Theology For Practical Christian Living

Cultivating a Closer Relationship with our Lord and Savior Christ Jesus

Dr. Kelvin M. McCune

Copyright © 2008 by Dr. Kelvin M. McCune

Theology For Practical Christian Living
Cultivating a Closer Relationship
with our Lord and Savior Christ Jesus
by Dr. Kelvin M. McCune

Printed in the United States of America

ISBN 978-1-60647-029-9

All rights reserved solely by the author. The author guarantees all contents are original and do not infringe upon the legal rights of any other person or work. No part of this book may be reproduced in any form without the permission of the author. The views expressed in this book are not necessarily those of the publisher.

Unless otherwise indicated, Bible quotations are taken from The King James Version of the Bible. Copyright © 1988 by Thomas Nelson Publishers.

www.xulonpress.com

This Book is Affectionately Dedicated

To my wife Jaiwantee and —our precious children
Joel, Lael, and Adel.

Table of Contents

PART ONE: INTRODUCTION xvii

    A. Purpose.. xvii
    B. General Structure.. xix
    C. Method of Use..xx

PART TWO: SEVEN MAJOR DOCTRINAL AREAS

    Chapter One: Theology (The Doctrine of God)...........23

        A. The Gospel of Jesus Christ...............................25
        B. The Names and Titles of God..........................30
        C. The Nature of God..55

    Chapter Two: Christology (The Doctrine of Christ)....73

        A. Names and Titles of Christ Jesus 74
        B. Divine Attributes of Christ Jesus....................131
        C. The Incarnation of Christ Jesus......................139

Chapter Three: Pneumatology (The Doctrine of
the Holy Spirit) 149

  A. The Nature and Work of the Holy Spirit........149
  B. The Personality of the Holy Spirit..................151
  C. The Activity of the Holy Spirit......................154
  D. Resisting the Holy Spirit...............................160
  E. The Holy Spirit and Christ Jesus....................163
  F. The Holy Spirit's Relationship with
     Mankind..167
  G. The Filling of the Holy Spirit.......................173
  H. The Deity of the Holy Spirit.........................180

Chapter Four: Ecclesiology (The Doctrine of
the Church)..185

  A. The Church..185
  B. The Meaning of the Church...........................187
  C. Spiritual Gifts in the Church 196
  D. The Spiritual Gifts to Believers.....................198
  E. The Church Ordinances.................................212

Chapter Five: Demonology (The Doctrine of Satan
and Demons) 217

  A. The Origin of Satan.......................................217
  B. Names and Descriptive Titles of Satan 220
  C. Satan's Limitations..227
  D. The Work of Satan...230
  E. The Origin of Demons...................................236
  F. The Characteristics of Demons......................237
  G The Work of Demons.....................................240
  H The Characteristics of Demon Possession 241
  I. The Destiny of Demons..................................243

Chapter Six: Soteriology (The Doctrine of Salvation)..................245

    A. The Need for Salvation 246
    B. God's Remedy for Sin 250
    C. The Conditions for Salvation 259
    D. The Eternal Security of the Believer..................263

Chapter Seven: Eschatology (The Doctrine of Future Events)..................267

    A. The Church Age 268
    B. The Rapture of the Church..................273
    C. The Judgment Seat of Christ..................275
    D. The Great Tribulation..................282
    E. The Antichrist..................286
    F. The Battle of Armageddon..................291
    G. The Return of Christ 293
    H. The Millennium..................300
    I. The Great White Throne Judgment 312
    J. The New Heaven and New Earth..................315
    K. The New Jerusalem..................315

PART THREE: PRINCIPLES FOR PRACTICAL CHRISTIAN LIVING

Chapter Eight: Christian Living..................321

    A. The Christians 321
    B. Our Need for a Savior 321
    C. The Christ..................323
    D. Salvation through Faith..................326
    E. The Christian Life..................328
    F. The New Nature 329
    G. The New Relationship..................329

Chapter Nine: Prayer 337

    A. What is Prayer? 337
    B. The Elements of Prayer 338
    C. Confession 341
    D. Intercession 344
    E. Petition 345

Chapter 10: Giving 351

    A. The Principles of Giving 351
    B. Financial Stewardship 355
    C. Greed 355
    D. Financial Planning 356
    E. Sharing with Others 357
    F. Your Family's Needs 358
    G. Savings 358
    H. Possessions 359

Chapter 11: Bible Study 363

    A. Reasons for Studying the Bible 363
    B. Keys to Effective Bible Study 368
    C. A Quiet Spirit 370
    D. The Benefits of Bible Study 371

Chapter 12: Victory over Satan 381

    A. Acknowledge Christ 382
    B. The Holy Spirit 386
    C. The Power of Prayer 389

Preface

This book is written to express the paramount importance of understanding systematic theology in a way that impacts the lives of believers on a daily basis. My passion is to encourage God's people to become Christ-centered with a dedicated and loyal heart to Him which will lead them to proclaim the gospel of Jesus Christ to a lost and dying world. Therefore, one motive for writing this book is to help believers to cultivate a closer relationship with our Lord Jesus Christ through the study of the Word of God. It is also my desire that unbelievers will come to know the Lord Jesus Christ as their Lord and Savior through reading this book.

My intent was to simplify this book so that it would be easy to read and understand. This is not taking away from Scripture, but teaching Scripture in such a way that people will appreciate the pure and unadulterated Word of God. My prayer is that believers will come to understand that God expects them to study and meditate in His Word daily and to apply His Word to their lives moment-by-moment. God has given us all things through His Word and the indwelling of the Holy Spirit to live holy lives in this sinful and adulterous world. Apostle Peter said, "According as His divine power hath given unto us all things that pertain unto life and godliness, through the knowledge of Him that hath called us to glory and virtue: Whereby are given unto us exceeding great and precious promises: that by these ye might be partakers of the divine nature, having escaped the corruption that is in the world through lust" (2 Pet. 1:3-4).

All Scripture is to reveal the Lord Jesus Christ. Therefore, this book was prayerfully written with the focus on the Lord Jesus Christ and with love, zeal and a commitment to worship and serve Him with my whole heart. It was also written to reveal Him in a unique way to the readers. It is hoped that the readers of this book will be instrumental in encouraging others to develop a desire to study the Word of God and to seek a greater knowledge of our Lord Jesus Christ through His Word. Apostle Peter commanded, "But grow in grace, and in the knowledge of our Lord and Savior Jesus Christ. To Him be glory both now and forever. Amen" (2 Pet. 3:18). The Lord Jesus said, "And thou shalt love the Lord thy God with all thy heart, and with all thy soul, and with all thy mind, and with all thy strength: this is the first commandment" (Mark 12:30). "Jesus answered and said unto him, If a man love Me, he will keep My words…" (John 14:23). One way to show our Lord Jesus that we love Him is by sharing His gospel as He commanded. "Go into all the world and preach the gospel to every creature" (Mark 16:15). Thus, another purpose of this book is to share the gospel to all who read it.

The entire world is being bombarded with false doctrines all the time. Hence, it is imperative that those who understand the true Word of God make a commitment to obey the Lord and to communicate His Word to those who are truly seeking to know the true and living God. God's Word was distorted by Satan in the Garden of Eden and he continues to distort God's Word to this very day. All readers are encouraged to prayerfully study God's Word as they read through this book. Satan does not want God's people to study the Word of God, because they will then know the truth and the truth will make them free. Jesus said, "And ye shall know the truth, and the truth shall make you free" (John 8:32).

I must emphasize that this book by no means substitutes the command by God to meditate in His Word day and night. This book should only drive readers to the Word of God. The Lord commands that we meditate in His Word day and night. The only way that believers will grow spiritually in their personal lives and ministries is to obey God. The Lord said to Joshua, "This book of the law shall not depart out of thy mouth; but thou shalt meditate therein day and night, that thou mayest observe to do according to all that is written therein: for then thou shalt make thy way prosperous, and then thou shalt have good success" (Joshua 1:8). In other words, Joshua would only be able to fulfill God's purpose for his life, that is, to bring the people into the Promised Land, if he obeyed God by meditating in God's Word daily. The Psalmist said that the believer's delight is in the law of the Lord, and in His law doth he meditate day and night (Ps. 1:2).

Moreover, this book will help believers to understand that many trials will be encountered when attempting to fulfill God's purpose for their lives. Being able to endure the trials of this life and becoming an "overcomer" as God works through believers to fulfill His purpose for their lives means that believers must feed on God's Word daily and must be willing to obey His Word. Jesus said, "Sanctify them through Thy truth: Thy word is truth" (John 17:17). The Lord Jesus promises the "crown of life" to those who endure and overcome the temptations of this world and the many schemes of the devil. James said, "Blessed is the man that endureth temptation: for when he is tried, he shall receive the crown of life, which the Lord hath promised to them that love Him" (James 1:12). In Revelation the Lord Jesus said, "Fear none of those things which thou shalt suffer: behold, the devil shall cast some of you into prison, that ye may be tried; and ye shall have tribulation ten days: be thou faithful unto death, and I will give thee a crown of life" (Rev. 2:10). As believers adhere to Christ's command to "Go into all the world and preach the gospel to every creature" (Mark 16:15), they will suffer persecution. Therefore, this book endeavors to help believers see God's plan and purpose for their lives and to realize that the devil stands ready to oppose the people of God on every front. Apostle Paul said, "Yea, and all that will live godly in Christ Jesus shall suffer persecution" (2 Tim. 3:12).

The Lord has used numerous people to impact my life for Christ's sake by influencing my commitment to teach God's Word and to become committed to missions and evangelism at home and in foreign lands. There are too many to mention, so I will say that I am so grateful for all of those whom God has used. Through the influencing of those individuals, God has used me in ministry around the world in Guyana, South America; Uganda, East Africa; the Congo, Kenya, Tanzania, Rwanda, India, Nigeria, Liberia, Amsterdam, and many other countries.

The material delineated in this book is another method in which God is using me to teach His people around the world. I pray that utilizing this book as a study tool will give the readers a greater desire to study God's Word and a greater commitment to our Lord Jesus Christ. I also pray that it will promote spiritual growth in the readers' personal lives and ministries as they use it in personal settings, in classroom settings and in small group settings. The ultimate aim of this book is to drive people to cultivate a closer walk with our Lord Jesus Christ and to proclaim the gospel of Jesus Christ and serve Him in a mighty way by bringing souls into His kingdom.

All praise and glory should be directed to Jesus Christ our Lord and Savior. To God be the glory for the great things which He has done. Amen.

Acknowledgement

Grateful acknowledgement is made to:
Minister Beatrice Y. Smith

INTRODUCTION

A. Purpose

There is a need today for Christians to grow in their awareness of fulfilling Christ's Great Commission. After accepting Christ Jesus as Lord and Savior, the believer has to grow spiritually. He has to understand basic Bible doctrine. He has to discover God's direction and purpose for his life. Furthermore, he has to seek to experience God's will being worked out in his life as he ministers to others.

This discipleship manual focuses on enabling believers to receive basic doctrine and guidance. Certainly it will not meet every spiritual need. Prayerfully it will encourage the believer to continue to desire the Word of God. God's Word is a lamp unto our feet and a light unto our path (Ps. 119:105).

Psalm 119:105

"*Thy word is a lamp unto my feet, and a light unto my path.*"

The language is kept simple. I avoided technical theological terms. Those that were necessary to use were well defined. This is not a technical theological thesis. It is a practical discipleship manual.

It is my intent to communicate these Biblical truths in the simplest way possible, and not taking away from their profound meanings. This discipleship manual can be used in any nation by any believer who can read. The purpose of this manual is to give help where it is most needed in light of spiritual warfare. Satan, the prince of this world, is stealing the Word of God from the hearts of men and women. One of his strategies is complicating or distorting God's truth. Therefore, with great conviction I seek to explain the following doctrine in a manner that will be spiritually helpful to my fellow saints.

This manual, therefore, is for Christians who desire to become more effective disciples of the Lord Jesus Christ. In writing, I defended no particular denominational tradition. I simply explained God's Word as taught in the Holy Scriptures. I have faith that God will use this manual to bear witness to Christ Jesus. The Word of God says that whatever we do, we are to do all to His glory (1 Cor. 10:31). My sincere prayer is that through the study of this manual, believers will become more effective disciples of Christ.

<u>1 Corinthians 10:31</u>

"Whether therefore ye eat, or drink, or whatsoever ye do, do all to the glory of God."

This study presupposes several matters: the writers of both the Old and the New Testaments were inspired by the Holy Spirit; the Holy Scripture is fully from God; it is infallible and inerrant in all respects (2 Tim. 3:16-17; 2 Pet. 1:20-21).

2 Timothy 3:16-17

"*All scripture is given by inspiration of God, and is profitable for doctrine, for reproof, for correction, for instruction in righteousness: That the man of God may be perfect, thoroughly furnished unto all good works.*"

2 Peter 1:20-21

"*Knowing this first, that no prophecy of the scripture is of any private interpretation. For the prophecy came not in old time by the will of man: but holy men of God spake as they were moved by the Holy Ghost.*"

B. General Structure

This manual consists of three sections. This first section presents introductory explanations. In the second section, seven major doctrinal areas will be considered:

- Theology
- Christology
- Pneumatology
- Ecclesiology
- Demonology
- Soteriology
- Eschatology

The third section deals with more practical issues. This is not to say that theology is not practical. However, the practical areas in this section will help the believer know how to apply doctrine in everyday life. This section covers five areas:

- Christian Living
- Prayer
- Giving
- Bible Study
- Victory over Satan

It should be noted that the order of the areas in each section is not based on its relative importance. All knowledge of God's Word is equally and significantly important.

C. Method of Use

Read carefully the area you are studying. Also read it prayerfully. As you come upon a Scripture text, search the Bible if you do not fully understand. Read the verses or chapters before and after the given Scripture reference. Remember that Scripture always interprets Scripture.

When you get to the question and answer section, read the question. Try to answer before looking at the answer given, and then compare your answer with the one in the manual. If in doubt, review the contents of the related area.

I believe that God has given His people a hunger for His Word. Pray and ask the Holy Spirit to nurture this hunger (Matt. 5:6). As we grow in knowledge of God's Word, we will live a triumphant life. We will live a life of usefulness to our Lord. Faith comes from hearing God's Word (Rom. 10:17).

Matthew 5:6

"Blessed are they which do hunger and thirst after righteousness: for they shall be filled."

Romans 10:17

"*So then faith cometh by hearing, and hearing by the Word of God.*"
We will become more Christlike as we grow to know Him (2 Pet. 3:18). Those who desire this abundant life will, prayerfully, be refreshed and stimulated by the messages in this manual.

2 Peter 3:18

"*But grow in grace, and in the knowledge of our Lord and Savior Jesus Christ. To him be glory both now and for ever. Amen.*"

Satan does not want us to grow spiritually. Praise God, however, for He is always giving us the victory over the enemy. As we mature in God's Word, we will be better able to discern the works of the devil. We will become knowledgeable of His desires. We will be able to experience victory over our battles.

I believe that this discipleship manual is more than doctrine. It is helping us to grow to know Christ. God will use His Word to fulfill His purpose. This manual is the result of many hours of prayer. It is written under the conviction of the Holy Spirit. I pray that all praise and glory will go to our Savior Christ Jesus. He is Lord. I believe that all Scripture is to reveal our Lord and Savior Christ Jesus.

Chapter 1

THEOLOGY

Theology is the study of the doctrine of God. The word is derived from the Greek word "theos" meaning God. The focus of theology, therefore, is the nature, attributes, purposes, and activity of God. It is important to be mindful that knowledge of God is a very humbling experience.

Theology is based on the supposition that God has revealed Himself to mankind. The basis for Christian theology is the Bible. The Bible is God's revealed truth to the world. Jesus said, "Sanctify them through thy truth: thy word is truth" (John 17:17). Second Timothy 3:16 states that all Scripture is God-breathed, that is, straight out of the mouth of God. Therefore, the Bible should not be looked upon as a book about God that was authored by men. The Bible must be viewed as God's revelation of Himself. Therefore, the focus of any study of God must center on the Bible. It is important to know that holy men of God wrote as they were moved by the Holy Spirit (2 Pet. 1:20-21).

John 17:17

> "Sanctify them through thy truth: thy word is truth."

2 Timothy 3:16

"*All scripture is given by inspiration of God, and is profitable for doctrine, for reproof, for correction, for instruction in righteousness.*"

2 Peter 1:20-21

"*Knowing this first, that no prophecy of the scripture is of any private interpretation. For the prophecy came not in old time by the will of man: but holy men of God spake as they were moved by the Holy Ghost.*"

Through a study of theology, one will learn that God has revealed Himself in three persons, yet it is clear that there is only one God. These three are the Father, the Son and the Holy Spirit. It is especially important to understand that all of Scripture focuses on the person and work of Jesus Christ. This is because He is God's perfect revelation of Himself to man (Heb. 1:3). As we study the Word of God, we will see in Jesus all that God reveals about Himself.

Hebrews 1:3

"*Who being the brightness of his glory, and the express image of his person, and upholding all things by the word of his power, when he had by himself purged our sins, sat down on the right hand of the Majesty on high.*"

John 14:6

"Jesus saith unto him, I am the way, the truth, and the life: no man cometh unto the Father, but by me."

A. The Gospel of Jesus Christ

<u>*1 Corinthians 2:14*</u>

"But the natural man receiveth not the things of the Spirit of God: for they are foolishness unto him: neither can he know them, because they are spiritually discerned."

True knowledge of God comes only through revelation by the Spirit of God (1 Cor. 2:10-12).

<u>*1 Corinthians 2:10-12*</u>

"But God hath revealed them unto us by his Spirit: for the Spirit searcheth all things, yea, the deep things of God. For what man knoweth the things of a man, save the spirit of man which is in him? even so the things of God knoweth no man, but the Spirit of God. Now we have received, not the spirit of the world, but the spirit which is of God; that we might know the things that are freely given to us of God."

This is because man cannot understand that which is spiritual unless it is revealed to him. In fact, one must be born again of the Spirit before he can begin to gain an understanding of a relationship with God. Therefore, one must begin with the Gospel of Jesus Christ in order to gain a true knowledge of God.

Genesis 1:27-29

> "So God created man in his own image, in the image of God created he him; male and female created he them. And God blessed them, and God said unto them, Be fruitful, and multiply, and replenish the earth, and subdue it: and have dominion over the fish of the sea, and over the fowl of the air, and over every living thing that moveth upon the earth. And God said, Behold, I have given you every herb bearing seed, which is upon the face of all the earth, and every tree, in the which is the fruit of a tree yielding seed; to you it shall be for meat."

Adam, the first man, was created in perfect harmony with God and nature. However, through disobedience, he became a sinner and an outlaw. He lost fellowship with God and suffered the curse of death (Gen. 3:17-19). His very nature changed so that he became incapable of pleasing God (Rom. 8:8).

Genesis 3:17-19

> "And unto Adam he said, Because thou hast hearkened unto the voice of thy wife, and hast eaten of the tree, of which I commanded thee, saying, Thou shalt not eat of it: cursed is the ground for thy sake; in sorrow shalt thou eat of it all the days of thy life; Thorns also and thistles shall it bring forth to thee; and thou shalt eat the herb of the field; In the sweat of thy face shalt thou eat

bread, till thou return unto the ground; for out of it wast thou taken: for dust thou art, and unto dust shalt thou return."

<u>Romans 8:8</u>

"So then they that are in the flesh cannot please God."

<u>Romans 5:12</u>

"Wherefore, as by one man sin entered into the world, and death by sin; and so death passed upon all men, for that all have sinned."

All people are descendents of Adam and inherited his sin nature, and also came under the curse of death. But God still loved man, so He provided a way in which man could be restored to fellowship with Him.

<u>Romans 5:8</u>

"But God commendeth his love toward us, in that, while we were yet sinners, Christ died for us."

God Himself came in the form of man to suffer death for the sins of man (Phil. 2:5-8). Jesus Christ redeemed man from the curse of sin by His death on the cross at Calvary (1 Pet. 1:18-19). It was His resurrection from the dead that proved that His death satisfied the debt of sin and removed the curse from us (1 Pet. 1:3).

<u>Philippians 2:5-8</u>

"Let this mind be in you, which was also in Christ Jesus: Who, being in the form of God, thought it not robbery to be equal with God: But made himself of no reputation, and took upon him the form of a servant, and was made in the likeness of men: And being found in fashion as a man, he humbled himself, and became obedient unto death, even the death of the cross."

<u>1 Peter 1:18-19</u>

"Forasmuch as ye know that ye were not redeemed with corruptible things, as silver and gold, from your vain conversation received by tradition from your fathers; But with the precious blood of Christ, as of a lamb without blemish and without spot."

<u>1 Peter 1:3</u>

"Blessed be the God and Father of our Lord Jesus Christ, which according to his abundant mercy hath begotten us again unto a lively hope by the resurrection of Jesus Christ from the dead."

<u>Romans 10:9, 13</u>

"That if thou shalt confess with thy mouth the Lord Jesus, and shalt believe in thine heart that God hath raised him from the dead, thou shalt be saved." "For whosoever shall call upon the name of the Lord shall be saved."

Salvation is free for the asking. It cannot be earned (Titus 3:5). When one responds to the Gospel, God blesses that person not only with eternal life, but also with the Holy Spirit who takes residence within that person (Eph. 1:13, 14). The Spirit of God begins to reveal the things of God to the born-again believer (1 Cor. 2:12). As he reads the Word of God, the Holy Spirit will give him understanding of the spiritual truths taught therein (John 16:13-15). Thus, the born-again believer grows in grace and knowledge of the Lord Jesus Christ and walks in fellowship with God. That is why one must believe the Gospel of Jesus Christ in order to gain true knowledge of God.

Titus 3:5

"Not by works of righteousness which we have done, but according to his mercy he saved us, by the washing of regeneration, and renewing of the Holy Ghost."

Ephesians 1:13-14

"In whom ye also trusted, after that ye heard the word of truth, the Gospel of your salvation: in whom also after that ye believed, ye were sealed with that Holy Spirit of promise, Which is the earnest of our inheritance until the redemption of the purchased possession, unto the praise of his glory."

1 Corinthians 2:12

"Now we have received, not the spirit of the world, but the spirit which is of God; that we

might know the things that are freely given to us of God."

<u>John 16:13-15</u>

"Howbeit when he, the Spirit of truth, is come, he will guide you into all truth: for he shall not speak of himself; but whatsoever he shall hear, that shall he speak: and he will show you things to come. He shall glorify me: for he shall receive of mine, and shall show it unto you. All things that the Father hath are mine: therefore said I, that he shall take of mine, and shall show it unto you."

B. The Names and Titles of God

In the Bible, God reveals truths about Himself by the names He ascribes to Himself. In order to understand the character, nature and purposes of God, we must have a proper understanding of His names. The three primary names of God are Elohim, Jehovah, and Adonai.

1. Elohim

<u>Genesis 1:1</u>

"In the beginning God (Elohim) created the heaven and the earth."

Elohim is a name of God that conveys the meaning of One having rule or great power. This name declares God to be a strong covenant-keeper, able to carry out His will and word by the might of His power. It is the first name God ascribes to Himself in His Word. In the King James Version of the Bible, this word is translated "God."

The word "Elohim" is the plural form of the word "El." Elohim refers to more than one person. This reveals to us that God exists as more than one personality. Genesis 1:26 is translated, "And God said, Let us make man in our image after to our likeness..." Verbs used with this name are singular, such as ". . . For I am God, and there is no other (Isa. 45:22b)." This supports the doctrine of the Trinity, that is, God has revealed Himself in the persons of the Father, the Son and the Holy Spirit. Yet it also declares the unity of God. These three are not three gods, but one God. Paul blesses us with the words, "The grace of the Lord Jesus Christ, and the love of God, and the communion of the Holy Spirit be with you all. Amen." (2 Cor. 13:14).

<u>Genesis 1:26a</u>

"And God said, Let us make man in our image, after our likeness..."

<u>Isaiah 45:22b</u>

"...for I am God (Elohim) and there is none else."

<u>2 Corinthians 13:14</u>

"The grace of the Lord Jesus Christ, and the love of God, and the communion of the Holy Ghost, be with you all. Amen."

We can have full confidence and assurance that God will carry out His promises to us because He is Elohim. The fact that He is Elohim is the basis of our faith. When Jesus says,

"Ye believe in God, believe also in me" (John 14:1), we understand that He is Elohim.

John 14:1

"Let not your heart be troubled: ye believe in God, believe also in me."

2. Jehovah (Yahweh)

Exodus 3:13-14

"And Moses said unto God, Behold, when I come unto the children of Israel, and shall say unto them, The God of your fathers hath sent me unto you; and they shall say to me, What is his name? what shall I say unto them? And God said unto Moses, I AM THAT I AM (Jehovah): and he said, Thus shalt thou say unto the children of Israel, I AM (Jehovah) hath sent me unto you."

God's personal name is represented in the Hebrew Scriptures by the letters, "YHWH." This is called the Tetragrammaton. This is God's personal name, and was considered so holy by the ancient Hebrews that they felt unworthy even to pronounce it. It is unclear how this name should be pronounced. Traditionally, the names "Jehovah" and "Yahweh" have been used in place of the Tetragrammaton in order to aid the modern reader in pronunciation. Most English translations use the word, "LORD," "LORD God," or "God."

1 Samuel 17:47

"And all this assembly shall know that the LORD saveth not with sword and spear: for the battle is the LORD's, and he will give you into our hands."

This name declares God to be "the Eternal Self-Existing One" and is used to demonstrate the sureness with which God will keep His Word. It also reflects on the unchangeableness or immutability of God. God is totally reliable because He does not change.

Numbers 23:19

"God is not a man, that he should lie; neither the son of man, that he should repent: hath he said, and shall he not do it? or hath he spoken, and shall he not make it good?"

Malachi 3:6a

"For I am the Lord, I change not…"

Hebrews 13:8

"Jesus Christ the same yesterday, and today, and for ever."

James 1:17

"Every good gift and every perfect gift is from above, and cometh down from the Father of lights, with whom is no variableness, neither shadow of turning."

3. Adonai

   Genesis 15:1-2

   "After these things the word of the LORD came unto Abram in a vision, saying, Fear not, Abram: I am thy shield, and thy exceeding great reward. And Abram said, Lord (Adonai) God, what wilt thou give me, seeing I go childless, and the steward of my house is this Eliezer of Damascus?"

The word "Adonai" means "master" or "owner". In the King James Version this word is translated "Lord" or "lord" in the Old Testament. It is used as a name of God, but also it is used in the secular sense for anyone who has authority, and as a greeting of respect much as "Sir" is used today in this sense. This name reveals God as Master and Owner. This is why we should approach God with reverence and respect. Jesus is our Adonai for He bought us with the price of His shed blood on the cross of Calvary.

   1 Corinthians 7:22-23

   "For he that is called in the Lord, being a servant is the Lord's freeman: likewise also he that is called, being free, is Christ's servant. Ye are bought with a price; be not ye the servants of men."

REVIEW

What Hebrew word is translated as "God"?

The Hebrew word Elohim is translated as "God." This name reveals God as the Eternal, Self-Existing One.

Since Elohim is plural in number, what does this tell us about God's divine nature?

This name reveals God as One who rules with great power and authority. It also shows that God exists as more than one personality. This supports the doctrine of the Trinity, that is, God has revealed Himself in the persons of the Father, the Son and the Holy Spirit. Although this is true, the name Elohim makes clear that there is only one God, not three.

What is the meaning of the name of God, "Jehovah"?

This name declares God to be "the Eternal, Self-Existing One." The name Jehovah is an English rendering for the personal name of God. In Hebrew Scriptures, that name is represented as "YHWH" and is referred to as the Tetragrammaton. It was never pronounced by the ancient Hebrews. The name Jehovah is used to aid modern readers in pronouncing God's name. In English translations, this name is translated "LORD," "LORD God," and "God."

What does the name "Adonai" declare God to be?

It declares that God is our Owner and Master, One who is due respect and obedience. This name also makes clear that we belong to God.

4. Compound Names of God

Throughout the Old Testament we find other names of God. These names are compound in structure and are usually combinations of one of the primary names of God with another name. These compound names reveal God in special ways. Let us now consider some of these names.

a. El Elyon

Genesis 14:18-20

> "And Melchizedek king of Salem brought forth bread and wine: and he was the priest of the most high God (El Elyon). And he blessed him, and said, Blessed be Abram of the most high God (El Elyon), possessor of heaven and earth: And blessed be the most high God (El Elyon), which hath delivered thine enemies into thy hand. And he gave him tithes of all."

This name combines the name "El" which means "strong one" with "Elyon" which means "most high." The name El Elyon reveals God as the "Most High Strong One" and conveys the sense that God, as the possessor of heaven and earth, is supreme over His creation and preeminent over all beings (Col. 1:17). It is a name that demands reverence and worship. Jesus, having been given all authority in heaven and on earth, is revealed to be our El Elyon.

Colossians 1:17

> "And he is before all things, and by him all things consist."

Matthew 28:18

"And Jesus came and spake unto them, saying, All power is given unto me in heaven and in earth."

b. El Roi

Genesis 16:13

"And she called the name of the LORD that spake unto her, Thou God seest me (El Roi): for she said, Have I also here looked after him that seeth me?"

This name means "the God who sees." From this name, we behold God as the One who is personally interested in our welfare. Hagar learned this during a time of great stress in her life. She left her home because of the harsh treatment at the hands of Sarai (Sarah), and was alone when God appeared to her. He blessed her with a son who was Abram's (Abraham's) first offspring. She was so comforted that she declared God to be "the One who sees" her. She learned that she was not alone for God was with her. We are not alone for Jesus is our El Roi. Jesus is our High Priest who lives to ever make intercession for us because He knows our weaknesses.

Hebrews 7:25

"Wherefore he is able also to save them to the uttermost that come unto God by him, seeing he ever liveth to make intercession for them."

2 Chronicles 16:9a

"For the eyes of the LORD run to and fro throughout the whole earth, to show himself strong in the behalf of them whose heart is perfect toward him."

Job 28:24

"For he looketh to the ends of the earth, and seeth under the whole heaven."

Job 31:4

"Doth not he see my ways, and count all my steps?"

Job 34:21

"For his eyes are upon the ways of man, and he seeth all his goings."

Job 36:7a

"He withdraweth not his eyes from the righteous."

Psalm 33:13-15

"The LORD looketh from heaven; he beholdeth all the sons of men. From the place of his habitation he looketh upon all the inhabitants of the earth. He fashioneth their hearts alike; he considereth all their works."

Psalm 33:18-19

"Behold, the eye of the LORD is upon them that fear him, upon them that hope in his mercy; To deliver their soul from death, and to keep them alive in famine."

Psalm 34:15

"The eyes of the LORD are upon the righteous, and his ears are open unto their cry."

Proverbs 5:21

"For the ways of man are before the eyes of the LORD, and he pondereth all his goings."

Proverbs 15:3

"The eyes of the LORD are in every place, beholding the evil and the good."

Jeremiah 16:17

"For mine eyes are upon all their ways: they are not hid from my face, neither is their iniquity hid from mine eyes."

Jeremiah 32:19

"Great in counsel, and mighty in work: for thine eyes are open upon all the ways of the sons of men: to give every one according to his ways, and according to the fruit of his doings."

c. El Shaddai

Genesis 17:1

"And when Abram was ninety years old and nine, the LORD appeared to Abram, and said unto him, I am the Almighty God (El Shaddai); walk before me, and be thou perfect."

This name is made up of two words: "El" means "strong one," and "Shaddai" means "strength-giver" or "the one who is able." This name declares God to be "the Almighty, all-sufficient God." This name made it clear to Abraham that nothing was beyond the power of God to perform for "with God all things are possible" (Matt. 19:26c).

We see Jesus as our El Shaddai for Paul declares, "I can do all things through Christ which strengtheneth me" (Phil. 4:13).

Matthew 19:26

"But Jesus beheld them, and said unto them, With men this is impossible; but with God all things are possible."

Philippians 4:13

"I can do all things through Christ which strengtheneth me."

Ephesians 3:20-21

"Now unto him that is able to do exceeding abundantly above all that we ask or think,

according to the power that worketh in us, Unto him be glory in the church by Christ Jesus throughout all ages, world without end. Amen."

REVIEW

What does the name "El Elyon" teach us about God?

This name reveals God as the possessor of heaven and earth. He is supreme over His creation and preeminent over all beings.

What does the name "El Roi" teach us about God?

The name "El Roi" means "the God who sees." It teaches us that God is personally interested in us and is a source of hope in times of troubles.

What does the name "El Shaddai" teach us about God?

The name "El Shaddai" reveals that God is "the Almighty, all-sufficient God" who is able to do above and beyond all that we can think or imagine.

    d. Jehovah-Jireh

<u>Genesis 22:13-14</u>

"And Abraham lifted up his eyes, and looked, and behold behind him a ram caught in a thicket by his horns: and Abraham went and took the ram, and offered him up for a burnt offering in the stead of his son. And Abraham called the name of that place Jehovah-Jireh

(The LORD will provide): as it is said to this day, In the mount of the LORD it shall be seen."

This name means "The LORD will provide." We know from this name that we lack no good thing. First of all, God provided us with a Savior. Just as God provided a ram as a substitute for Abraham's son, Isaac, God sent Jesus to die on the cross for our sins as our substitute. He also promises that if we seek His kingdom and His righteousness, He will provide all our needs (Matt. 6:33).

<u>Matthew 6:33</u>

"But seek ye first the kingdom of God, and his righteousness; and all these things shall be added unto you."

<u>Psalm 34:8-10</u>

"O taste and see that the LORD is good: blessed is the man that trusteth in him. O fear the LORD, ye his saints: for there is no want to them that fear him. The young lions do lack, and suffer hunger: but they that seek the LORD shall not want any good thing."

<u>Psalm 84:11</u>

"For the LORD God is a sun and shield: the LORD will give grace and glory: no good thing will he withhold from them that walk uprightly."

John 3:16

"For God so loved the world, that he gave his only begotten Son, that whosoever believeth in him should not perish, but have everlasting life."

e. Jehovah-Rapha

Exodus 15:26

"And said, If thou wilt diligently hearken to the voice of the LORD thy God, and wilt do that which is right in his sight, and wilt give ear to his commandments, and keep all his statutes, I will put none of these diseases upon thee, which I have brought upon the Egyptians: for I am the LORD that healeth thee" (Jehovah-Rapha).

1 Peter 2:24

"Who his own self bare our sins in his own body on the tree, that we, being dead to sins, should live unto righteousness: by whose stripes ye were healed."

This name means "the LORD who heals." God promised to preserve the Hebrews from diseases if they would obey and serve Him. This promise has been fulfilled for us in Christ. Because Christ died for our sins, we have been healed from the sickness of sin. We look forward to the time when we will be freed from all effects of sin, even death (Rev. 21:4). Our Lord Jesus is our Jehovah-Rapha.

Revelation 21:4

"And God shall wipe away all tears from their eyes; and there shall be no more death, neither sorrow, nor crying, neither shall there be any more pain: for the former things are passed away."

  f. Jehovah-Nissi

Exodus 17:15

"And Moses built an altar, and called the name of it Jehovah-Nissi (The LORD is my banner)."

The name "Jehovah-Nissi" reveals that God gives us victory in spiritual warfare. It is not our own strength that enables us to resist temptation and which sustains us through trials. This strength comes only from God. Our Lord Christ Jesus is our banner of victory.

1 Corinthians 15:57

"But thanks be to God, which giveth us the victory through our Lord Jesus Christ."

2 Corinthians 2:14a

"Now thanks be unto God, which always causeth us to triumph in Christ."

g. Jehovah-Qadarh

Leviticus 20:8

"*And ye shall keep my statutes, and do them: I am the LORD (Jehovah-Qadarh) which sanctify you.*"

This name teaches us that God has sanctified us for Himself and for His purposes. To "sanctify" means "to set apart." God has set us apart from the world and called us to be holy (Ps. 4:3a). However, He does not leave it up to us. God performs a work in us which He promises to complete (Philip. 1:6). He makes us a new creation that is born of the Holy Spirit (2 Cor. 5:17). He gives us a spirit that is created in righteousness and true holiness (Eph. 4:24). Through His Word, He renews our minds (John 17:17) and equips us with spiritual armor to withstand the attacks of Satan (Eph. 6:10-18). All this is made possible by Christ Jesus who died for all our sins.

Psalm 4:3a

"*But know that the Lord hath set apart him that is godly for himself.*"

Philippians 1:6

"*Being confident of this very thing, that he which hath begun a good work in you will perform it until the day of Jesus Christ.*"

2 Corinthians 5:17

"Therefore if any man be in Christ, he is a new creature: old things are passed away; behold, all things are become new."

Ephesians 4:24

"And that ye put on the new man, which after God is created in righteousness and true holiness."

John 17:17

"Sanctify them through thy truth: thy word is truth."

Ephesians 6:10-18

"Finally, my brethren, be strong in the Lord, and in the power of his might. Put on the whole armor of God, that ye may be able to stand against the wiles of the devil. For we wrestle not against flesh and blood, but against principalities, against powers, against the rulers of the darkness of this world, against spiritual wickedness in high places. Wherefore take unto you the whole armor of God, that ye may be able to withstand in the evil day, and having done all, to stand. Stand therefore, having your loins girt about with truth, and having on the breastplate of righteousness; And your feet shod with the preparation of the Gospel of peace; Above all, taking the shield of faith, wherewith ye shall be able to *quench all the fiery darts of the wicked. And take the helmet of salvation, and the sword of the Spirit, which is the Word of God: Praying always with all prayer and supplication in the Spirit, and watching thereunto with all perseverance and supplication for all saints."*

<u>Hebrews 10:9-10</u>

"Then said He, Lo, I come to do thy will, O God. He taketh away the first, that He may establish the second. By the which will we are sanctified through the offering of the body of Jesus Christ once for all."

    h. Jehovah-Shalom

<u>Judges 6:23-24</u>

"And the LORD said unto him, Peace be unto thee; fear not: thou shalt not die. Then Gideon built an altar there unto the LORD, and called it Jehovah-shalom (the Lord Shalom): unto this day it is yet in Ophrah of the Abiezrites."

This name means "the LORD our Peace." Because of sin, we were enemies of God and condemned to death. Through Christ Jesus our Lord, we have peace with God (Rom. 5:1). His death satisfied God's judgment of sin and reconciled us with God (Rom. 5:10-11). The peace we have from God is the assurance that we can commune with Him in fellowship. The world does not know this kind of peace — their peace is merely a lull between hostilities and is accompanied by fear. The peace of God is eternal and all-encompassing.

Romans 5:1

"Therefore being justified by faith, we have peace with God through our Lord Jesus Christ."

Romans 5:10-11

"For if, when we were enemies, we were reconciled to God by the death of his Son, much more, being reconciled, we shall be saved by his life. And not only so, but we also joy in God through our Lord Jesus Christ, by whom we have now received the atonement."

John 14:27

"Peace I leave with you, my peace I give unto you: not as the world giveth, give I unto you. Let not your heart be troubled, neither let it be afraid."

i. Jehovah-Sabaoth

1 Samuel 1:3a

"And this man went up out of his city yearly to worship and to sacrifice unto the LORD of hosts (Jehovah-Sabaoth), in Shiloh."

James 5:4

"Behold, the hire of the laborers who have reaped down your fields, which is of you kept back by fraud, crieth: and the cries of them *which have reaped are entered into the ears of the Lord of Sabaoth."*

This name means "the LORD of hosts." With this name God reveals Himself as the Commander-in-Chief of armies of spiritual hosts arrayed to do battle with His enemies for the protection of His people. God is omnipotent, that is, He is all powerful. With this name, God reminds us that He fights our battles and avenges the wrongs done to His people.

1 Samuel 17:45

"Then said David to the Philistine, Thou comest to me with a sword, and with a spear, and with a shield: but I come to thee in the name of the LORD of hosts (Jehovah-Sabaoth), the God of the armies of Israel, whom thou hast defied."

Jeremiah 32:18

"Thou showest lovingkindness unto thousands, and recompensest the iniquity of the fathers into the bosom of their children after them: the Great, the Mighty God, the LORD of hosts (Jehovah-Sabaoth), is his name."

Romans 12:19

"Beloved, do not avenge yourselves, but rather give place to wrath; for it is written, Vengeance is Mine, I will repay, says the Lord."

j. Jehovah-Shammah

Ezekiel 48:35

"It was round about eighteen thousand measures: and the name of the city from that day shall be, The LORD is there (Jehovah-Shammah)."

Joshua 1:9

"Have not I commanded thee? Be strong and of a good courage; be not afraid, neither be thou dismayed: for the LORD thy God is with thee whithersoever thou goest."

This name means "the Lord is there." It teaches us that God is never far away. This knowledge gives us courage (Deut. 31:6). He is near so that we may enjoy sweet fellowship with Him and have freedom from fear. Our Lord Christ Jesus is our Jehovah-Shammah for He promised to be with us always (Matt. 28:20).

Deuteronomy 31:6

"Be strong and of a good courage, fear not, nor be afraid of them: for the Lord thy God, he it is that doth go with thee; he will not fail thee, nor forsake thee."

Matthew 28:20

"...and, lo, I am with you alway, even unto the end of the world. Amen."

Hebrews 13:5b-6

"For He hath said, I will never leave thee, nor forsake thee. So that we may boldly say, The LORD is my helper, and I will not fear what man shall do unto me."

Isaiah 41:10

"Fear thou not; for I am with thee: be not dismayed; for I am thy God: I will strengthen thee; yea, I will help thee; yea, I will uphold thee with the right hand of my righteousness."

k. Jehovah-Tsidkenu

Jeremiah 23:5-6

"Behold, the days come, saith the Lord, that I will raise unto David a righteous Branch, and a King shall reign and prosper, and shall execute judgment and justice in the earth. In his days Judah shall be saved, and Israel shall dwell safely: and this is his name whereby he shall be called, THE LORD OUR RIGHTEOUSNESS (Jehovah-Tsidkenu)."

Hebrews 4:15

"For we have not an high priest which cannot be touched with the feeling of our infirmities; but was in all points tempted like as we are, yet without sin."

1 Peter 1:15-16

"But as he which hath called you is holy, so be ye holy in all manner of conversation; Because it is written, Be ye holy; for I am holy."

This name means "The LORD our Righteousness." From this name we understand that true holiness comes from God and not a product of our self-efforts. From the Bible we know that everyone is born a sinner and alienated from God. However, through Christ we are born with a new nature that is righteous and holy. God calls us to holy living because His righteous character demands this. He chastens us to teach us to refrain from all forms of uncleanness and unrighteousness. Our Lord Christ Jesus is our Jehovah-Tsidkenu. It was because of His holiness that He could be our substitute on the cross.

1 Corinthians 1:30

"But of him are ye in Christ Jesus, who of God is made unto us wisdom, and righteousness, and sanctification, and redemption."

2 Corinthians 5:21

"For he hath made him to be sin for us, who knew no sin; that we might be made the righteousness of God in him."

l. Jehovah-Rohi

Psalm 23:1

"The LORD is my Shepherd; I shall not want."

This name means "The Lord my Shepherd." As Jehovah-Rohi God guides and cares for His people. A shepherd leads his flock to safety and refreshment. In the same way, God takes care of His people. Knowing this, we can turn to God for guidance and wisdom. Jesus identified Himself as the good Shepherd who lays down His life for His sheep (John 10:11). For us, He is our Jehovah-Rohi.

John 10:11

"I am the good shepherd. The good shepherd gives His life for the sheep."

REVIEW

What is the significance of the name "Jehovah-Jireh"?

This is the name by which we know God as the One who provides for our needs.

What is the meaning of the name "Jehovah-Qadarh"?

It means "The LORD that sanctifies." God has set us apart for Himself and for His purposes.

As sanctified persons, how are believers to live?

God has sanctified believers to live holy lives.

What does the word "shalom" mean?

The word "shalom" means "peace." God is known as Jehovah-Shalom because He has reconciled us to Himself through the blood of Jesus Christ.

What does the name "Jehovah-Sabaoth" mean?

It means "The LORD of hosts." Jehovah-Sabaoth has arrayed all His spiritual forces for the protection of His people. He will avenge the wrongs they suffer in due time.

What does the name "Jehovah-Shammah" mean?

This name means "The LORD is there." By this name, believers have assurance that God is always there in time of need.

What promise has Jesus given us as we go out to tell others about Him?

Jesus has promised that He is with us always, even to the end of the age.

What is the meaning of the name "Jehovah-Rapha"?

It means "The LORD that heals." By faith in Christ Jesus, we are healed of the curse sin brought upon us.

How does our Lord Christ Jesus declare Himself as Jehovah-Rapha?

By His shed blood on Calvary He has healed us from all our unrighteousness.

Since our God whom we serve is holy and righteous, how does He expect us to live?

He expects us to live holy and righteous lives.

What is the meaning of the name "Jehovah-Nissi"?

This name reveals that God gives us victory in spiritual warfare. It is not our strength that enables us to resist temptation and which sustains us through trials. This strength comes only from God. Our Lord Christ Jesus is our banner of victory.

What is the meaning of the name "Jehovah-Tsidkenu"?

It means "The Lord our Righteousness."

What is the meaning of "Jehovah-Rohi"?

This name means "The Lord my Shepherd."

C. The Nature of God

As we increase in our knowledge of God through His Word, we should be moved to worship Him. The psalmist has said, "Such knowledge is too wonderful for me" (Ps. 139:6).

Psalm 139:6

"Such knowledge is too wonderful for me; it is high, I cannot attain unto it."

The essential nature of God is that of Spirit. He is a Being who possesses intelligence, self-awareness, and will. However, He does not have a physical body nor is He composed of physical elements. He is apart from the physical world, yet He is seen in and known by the physical world. Romans 1:20 states, "For the invisible things of Him from the creation of the world are clearly seen, being understood by the things that are made, even His eternal power and Godhead..." Therefore, His divine attributes are evident to all.

<u>Romans 1:20</u>

"For the invisible things of him from the creation of the world are clearly seen, being understood by the things that are made, even his eternal power and Godhead; so that they are without excuse."

God has essential attributes that describe His abilities to carry out His will. He also possesses moral attributes that shape His will. Some of these are as follows:

1. God's Essential Attributes

    a. God is omnipotent.

<u>Revelation 19:6</u>

"And I heard as it were the voice of a great multitude, and as the voice of many waters, and as the voice of mighty thunderings, saying, Alleluia: for the Lord God omnipotent reigneth."

Matthew 19:26

"But Jesus beheld them, and said unto them, With men this is impossible; but with God all things are possible."

The word "omnipotent" means "all-powerful" or "possessing all power." The fact that God created the heavens and the earth demonstrates His omnipotence. God does not derive His power from any source; it is inherent in His nature. His power is supreme, that is, nothing can challenge or thwart it. He is the source of all power. Because He is omnipotent, God has total ability to do all that He desires. Our Lord Jesus is omnipotent.

Matthew 28:18

"And Jesus came and spake unto them, saying, All power is given unto Me in heaven and in earth."

b. God is omniscient.

1 John 3:20

"For if our heart condemn us, God is greater than our heart, and knoweth all things."

Omniscience means having all knowledge. God demonstrates that He has all knowledge by His acts of creation. His intimate and complete knowledge of man is made plain by the fact that He will judge all men according to their deeds (Rev. 20:12). God indeed wants us to acknowledge His omniscience because we need to trust that He is in control and that His way is best. This is what Job learned when God revealed to him the vastness and superiority of His knowledge as evidenced by the wonders of the universe and nature (Job 42:1-6).

Revelation 20:12

"And I saw the dead, small and great, stand before God; and the books were opened: and another book was opened, which is the Book of Life: and the dead were judged out of those things which were written in the books, according to their works."

Job 42:1-6

"Then Job answered the Lord, and said, I know that thou canst do every thing, and that no thought can be withholden from thee. Who is he that hideth counsel without knowledge? therefore have I uttered that I understood not; things too wonderful for me, which I knew not. Hear, I beseech thee, and I will speak: I will demand of thee, and declare thou unto me. I have heard of thee by the hearing of the ear: but now mine eye seeth thee. Wherefore I abhor myself, and repent in dust and ashes."

We must trust God even when we do not understand His ways because He is omniscient. His omniscience is seasoned with love so we can be assured that His way is best for us.

c. God is omnipresent.

Psalm 139:7-8

"Whither shall I go from Thy Spirit? or whither shall I flee from Thy presence? If I ascend up into heaven, Thou art there: if I make my bed in hell, behold, Thou art there."

Matthew 28:20

"...and, lo, I am with you alway, even unto the end of the world. Amen."

Hebrews 13:5b

"...for He hath said, "I will never leave thee, nor forsake thee..."

Omnipresent means being present everywhere. God's presence is real in every part of His creation. This is our assurance that He is in control. We are never alone, and we can be sure of His care and guidance always. The realization that God is omnipresent also should make us careful about what we say and do.

d. God is eternal.

Deuteronomy 33:27a

"The eternal God is thy refuge, and underneath are the everlasting arms."

John 1:1

"In the beginning was the Word, and the Word was with God, and the Word was God."

Revelation 1:18

"I am He that liveth, and was dead; and, behold, I am alive for evermore, Amen; and have the keys of hell and of death."

We naturally fear and dread death. The fact that God is eternal gives us hope of victory over death. We have the promise of eternal life with God. This knowledge should spur us to do good works because we have an eternal reward.

John 3:16

"For God so loved the world, that He gave his only begotten Son, that whosoever believeth in Him should not perish, but have everlasting life."

1 John 5:11-12

"And this is the record, that God hath given to us eternal life, and this life is in His Son. He that hath the Son hath life; and he that hath not the Son of God hath not life."

John 5:24

"Verily, verily, I say unto you, He that heareth my word, and believeth on Him that sent Me, hath everlasting life, and shall not come into

condemnation; but is passed from death unto life."

e. God is immutable.

<u>*Malachi 3:6a*</u>

"For I am the LORD, I change not."

<u>*Hebrews 13:8*</u>

"Jesus Christ the same yesterday, and today, and for ever."

We can totally trust God because He does not change. God's Word never changes; we can build our lives on it. We can be sure of His promises because they stand forever. We can truly know Him for He never changes.

2. God's Moral Attributes

   a. God is holy.

<u>*Leviticus 19:2*</u>

"Speak unto all the congregation of the children of Israel, and say unto them, Ye shall be holy: for I the LORD your God am holy."

<u>*Leviticus 20:26*</u>

"And ye shall be holy unto Me: for I the Lord am holy, and have severed you from other people, that ye should be Mine."

1 John 3:5

"And ye know that He was manifested to take away our sins; and in Him is no sin."

The holiness of God means that there is no evil in Him. God has no wicked ways. Purity is the hallmark of His character. His holiness is His glory for which He is due praise. Because of His holiness, we can trust God to lead us out of the muck of sin and impart His holiness in us.

Numbers 15:40

"That ye may remember, and do all my commandments, and be holy unto your God."

Ephesians 1:4

"According as He hath chosen us in Him before the foundation of the world, that we should be holy and without blame before Him in love."

Ephesians 5:27

"That He might present it to Himself a glorious church, not having spot, or wrinkle, or any such thing; but that it should be holy and without blemish."

1 Peter 1:15-16

"But as he which hath called you is holy, so be ye holy in all manner of conversation; Because it is written, Be ye holy; for I am holy."

b. God is righteous.

Psalm 7:9

"Oh let the wickedness of the wicked come to an end; but establish the just: for the righteous God trieth the hearts and reins."

1 John 2:1

"...And if any man sin, we have an advocate with the Father, Jesus Christ the righteous."

Righteousness is that quality by which one acts in a morally justifiable manner. God is righteous, and He demands that we live righteously. However, He blesses us by imparting His righteousness in us.

Romans 3:21-22

"But now the righteousness of God without the law is manifested, being witnessed by the law and the prophets; Even the righteousness of God which is by faith of Jesus Christ unto all and upon all them that believe: for there is no difference."

Isaiah 11:4

"But with righteousness shall He judge the poor, and reprove with equity for the meek of the earth: and He shall smite the earth with the rod of His mouth, and with the breath of His lips shall he slay the wicked."

Revelation 19:11

"And I saw heaven opened, and behold a white horse; and He that sat upon him was called Faithful and True, and in righteousness he doth judge and make war."

c. God is merciful.

1 Chronicles 16:34

"O give thanks unto the LORD; for he is good; for his mercy endureth for ever."

Psalm 86:13a

"For great is thy mercy toward me."

Psalm 136:26

"O give thanks unto the God of heaven: for his mercy endureth for ever."

Hebrews 2:17

"Wherefore in all things it behoved Him to be made like unto His brethren, that He might be a merciful and faithful high priest in things pertaining to God, to make reconciliation for the sins of the people."

God did not give us what we deserved for our sins; He forgave us and cleansed us from all unrighteousness. A propitiation is that which satisfies or wins favor. Christ's death is a propitiation for our sins because it satisfied God's judgment of sin and regained a peace with Him (Rom. 3:24-26; 1 John 2:2).

> ### Romans 3:24-26
>
> *"Being justified freely by his grace through the redemption that is in Christ Jesus: Whom God hath set forth to be a propitiation through faith in His blood, to declare His righteousness for the remission of sins that are past, through the forbearance of God; To declare, I say, at this time His righteousness: that He might be just, and the justifier of him which believeth in Jesus."*
>
> ### 1 John 2:2
>
> *"And he is the propitiation for our sins: and not for ours only, but also for the sins of the whole world."*
>
> ### Psalm 145:8
>
> *"The LORD is gracious, and full of compassion; slow to anger, and of great mercy."*
>
> ### Lamentations 3:22
>
> *"It is of the LORD's mercies that we are not consumed, because His compassions fail not."*

Ephesians 2:4

"But God, who is rich in mercy, for his great love wherewith he loved us."

Titus 3:5

"...but according to his mercy he saved us..."

d. God is faithful.

Deuteronomy 7:9

"Know therefore that the LORD thy God, he is God, the faithful God, which keepeth covenant and mercy with them that love him and keep his commandments to a thousand generations."

Hebrews 2:17

"Wherefore in all things it behoved him to be made like unto his brethren, that he might be a merciful and faithful high priest in things pertaining to God, to make reconciliation for the sins of the people."

    The Bible contains an extensive record of God's faithfulness to His Word and to His people. God does what He says He is going to do. Therefore, he is totally trustworthy and worthy of our faith. It is because of His faithfulness that we have hope of eternal glory.

1 Corinthians 1:9

"God is faithful, by whom ye were called unto the fellowship of his Son Jesus Christ our Lord."

1 Corinthians 10:13

"There hath no temptation taken you but such as is common to man: but God is faithful, who will not suffer you to be tempted above that ye are able; but will with the temptation also make a way to escape, that ye may be able to bear it."

1 Thessalonians 5:24

"Faithful is He that calleth you, who also will do it."

2 Thessalonians 3:3

"But the Lord is faithful, who shall stablish you, and keep you from evil."

2 Timothy 2:13

"If we believe not, yet he abideth faithful: he cannot deny himself."

1 John 1:9

"If we confess our sins, He is faithful and just to forgive us our sins, and to cleanse us from all unrighteousness."

Revelation 19:11

"And I saw heaven opened, and behold a white horse; and he that sat upon him was called Faithful and True, and in righteousness he doth judge and make war."

    e. God is good.

Nahum 1:7

"The LORD is good, a strong hold in the day of trouble; and He knoweth them that trust in Him."

Psalm 145:9

"The LORD is good to all, and His tender mercies are over all His works."

John 10:11

"I am the good shepherd. The good shepherd gives His life for the sheep."

    God bestows His blessings on all people. When we think of the things God has done for us even while we were rebelling against Him, we should be moved with a deeper love for Him. It was a realization of God's goodness in providing us with a Savior that led us to repent of our sins and believe on Jesus for salvation (Rom. 2:4).

Romans 2:4

"Or despisest thou the riches of his goodness and forbearance and longsuffering; not knowing that the goodness of God leadeth thee to repentance?"

f. God is long-suffering.

Exodus 34:6

"And the Lord passed by before him, and proclaimed, The Lord, The Lord God, merciful and gracious, longsuffering, and abundant in goodness and truth."

Nehemiah 9:17

"And refused to obey, neither were mindful of thy wonders that thou didst among them; but hardened their necks, and in their rebellion appointed a captain to return to their bondage: but thou art a God ready to pardon, gracious and merciful, slow to anger, and of great kindness, and forsookest them not."

Romans 2:3-4

"And thinkest thou this, O man, that judgest them which do such things, and doest the same, that thou shalt escape the judgment of God? Or despisest thou the riches of his goodness and forbearance and longsuffering; not knowing that the goodness of God leadeth thee to repentance?"

It is only because of God's long-suffering that He has not brought judgment on the world as yet. We ought to appreciate the fact that God gave us time to repent of our sins.

<u>2 Peter 3:9</u>

"The Lord is not slack concerning his promise, as some men count slackness; but is longsuffering to us-ward, not willing that any should perish, but that all should come to repentance."

REVIEW

What are the essential attributes of God?

The essential attributes of God are:

- Omnipotence - God is all-powerful.
- Omniscience - God knows all things.
- Omnipresence - God is present everywhere.
- Eternalness - God has no beginning or end.
- Immutability - God does not change.

What are the moral attributes of God?

The moral attributes of God are:

- Holiness - God is pure and without sin.
- Righteousness - God is totally and morally justified in His actions.
- Mercifulness - God is compassionate to those in need.

Faithfulness - God is true to His Word and totally reliable.
Goodness - God blesses all people regardless of their state.
Long-suffering - God is patient with sinners.

Chapter 2

CHRISTOLOGY

Christology is the study of the person and work of Jesus Christ. Christians ought to have a special interest in Christology because we are called to be servants of our Lord Christ Jesus. Through Christology, the Holy Spirit can cause us to grow in our knowledge of Christ, to experience the power of His resurrection in daily living, and to partake of the fellowship of His suffering with continual joy and peace. This helps us to become conformed to Christ's death, that is, to experience the continual fulfillment of Christ's purpose in our lives more than our own desires. It means less of us and more of Him. It means asking Him in prayer always, "Lord what is your will for my life today?" A study of Christology will cause us to experience such growth, and to love and serve Him. In 2 Corinthians 4:5, Paul reminds us that our main purpose for living is to proclaim Christ Jesus the Lord. We are chosen by God to be ambassadors for Christ, and empowered by the Holy Spirit to do the works that glorify Christ Jesus our Lord. May the Lord be magnified in our hearts and take us closer to His cross.

2 Corinthians 4:5

"For we preach not ourselves, but Christ Jesus the Lord; and ourselves your servants for Jesus' sake."

A. Names and Titles of Christ Jesus

1. Jesus

    Matthew 1:21

    "And she shall bring forth a son, and thou shalt call his name JESUS: for he shall save his people from their sins."

    Luke 1:31-33

    "And, behold, thou shalt conceive in thy womb, and bring forth a son, and shalt call his name JESUS. He shall be great, and shall be called the Son of the Highest: and the Lord God shall give unto him the throne of his father David: And he shall reign over the house of Jacob for ever; and of his kingdom there shall be no end."

    Luke 2:21

    "And when eight days were accomplished for the circumcising of the child, his name was called JESUS, which was so named of the angel before he was conceived in the womb."

This is the personal name of our Lord. It is the name He took for His earthly ministry. To Christians, this name not only identifies the historical Jesus, but also proclaims Him as Lord and Savior.

The name Jesus is the Greek form for the Hebrew name Joshua. Both names, Jesus and Joshua, mean "Jehovah our Savior." The name Jesus is found in the New Testament 683 times. This personal name of our Lord proclaims the humiliation of suffering; of sorrow He suffered in dying for the sins of the world. Jesus came and died so that whoever believes in Him may not perish, but have everlasting life (John 3:16). He is the Savior of the world. The name Jesus also reveals His greatness as Lord and King since He is clearly identified as Jehovah God.

John 3:16

"For God so loved the world, that he gave his only begotten Son, that whosoever believeth in him should not perish, but have everlasting life."

Acts 4:12

"Neither is there salvation in any other: for there is none other name under heaven given among men, whereby we must be saved."

1 Timothy 2:5-6

"For there is one God, and one mediator between God and men, the man Christ Jesus; Who gave himself a ransom for all, to be testified in due time."

Philippians 2:5-11

"Let this mind be in you, which was also in Christ Jesus: Who, being in the form of God, thought it not robbery to be equal with God: But made himself of no reputation, and took upon him the form of a servant, and was made in the likeness of men: And being found in fashion as a man, he humbled himself, and became obedient unto death, even the death of the cross. Wherefore God also hath highly exalted him, and given him a name which is above every name: That at the name of Jesus every knee should bow, of things in heaven, and things in earth, and things under the earth; And that every tongue should confess that Jesus Christ is Lord, to the glory of God the Father."

1 John 4:15

"Whosoever shall confess that Jesus is the Son of God, God dwelleth in him, and he in God."

2. Christ

Matthew 16:15-16

"He saith unto them, But whom say ye that I am? And Simon Peter answered and said, Thou art the Christ, the Son of the living God."

This name is the official title of the Son of God. The name Christ means "Anointed One." Our Lord Jesus is anointed as Prophet, Priest and King. The name Christ appears 312 times in the New Testament. In the four gospels, it appears only 56 times, while in the remainder of the New Testament it appears 256 times. On the other hand, the name Jesus appears 612 times in the four gospels, and in the remainder of the New Testament it appears 71 times. The reason why the name Jesus appears more times in the four gospels is because this name reveals His humanity and purpose, which was to suffer on Calvary's cross. The reason why the name Christ appears more in the rest of the New Testament than in the gospels is that this name reveals His anointed position as Prophet, Priest and King.

REVIEW

What is the meaning of the name Jesus?

The name Jesus means "the Lord is Salvation" or "Jehovah our Savior."

What is the Hebrew name for Jesus?

The Hebrew name for Jesus is Joshua.

What does the name "Jesus" proclaim about Him?

The name "Jesus" proclaims the truth that He suffered and died for the sins of the world.

What does the name "Christ" mean?

The name "Christ" means "Anointed One." To be anointed means to be chosen or commissioned for special service.

To what offices did God the Father anoint Christ Jesus?

Christ Jesus was anointed by God the Father to be a Prophet, Priest and King.

---

3. The Anointed Prophet

Acts 3:22-24

> "For Moses truly said unto the fathers, A prophet shall the Lord your God raise up unto you of your brethren, like unto me; him shall ye hear in all things whatsoever he shall say unto you. And it shall come to pass, that every soul, which will not hear that prophet, shall be destroyed from among the people. Yea, and all the prophets from Samuel and those that follow after, as many as have spoken, have likewise foretold of these days."

God called Samuel to be a prophet in the nation of Israel. As a prophet, he declared God's will and purpose to the people through prophecies. Samuel's office was temporary and ended with his death.

God gave prophecies in order to lead the people back to a right relationship with Him. Because He is the Mediator between God and man (1 Tim. 2:5), Jesus is the only means by which man can be reconciled or brought into a right relationship with God. Therefore the primary focus of all prophecy is Jesus Christ.

1 Timothy 2:5

"For there is one God, and one mediator between God and men, the man Christ Jesus."

Our Lord has been anointed Prophet by the Father. As such, He has completely revealed God's nature, character and purpose for mankind. No one can know God apart from Christ. Through His Word and His Church, He continues to reveal God to the world. Christ is a Prophet forever because, having been raised from the dead, He lives evermore.

Deuteronomy 18:15-19

"The Lord thy God will raise up unto thee a Prophet from the midst of thee, of thy brethren, like unto me; unto him ye shall hearken;...I will raise them up a Prophet from among their brethren, like unto thee, and will put my words in his mouth; and he shall speak unto them all that I shall command him. And it shall come to pass, that whosoever will not hearken unto my words which he shall speak in my name, I will require it of him."

REVIEW

Who was Samuel and why was he important?

Samuel was a prophet to the nation of Israel. He declared God's will and purpose to the people.

Why did God give prophecies?

God gave prophecies to lead people back to a right relationship with Him.

What is the central focus of all prophecy?

The central focus of all prophecy is Jesus Christ. This is true because He is the only means by which one can have a right relationship with God.

4. The Anointed High Priest

> *Hebrews 4:14-15*
>
> *"Seeing then that we have a great high priest, that is passed into the heavens, Jesus the Son of God, let us hold fast our profession. For we have not an high priest which cannot be touched with the feeling of our infirmities; but was in all points tempted like as we are, yet without sin."*

All the priests of the Old Testament were of the tribe of Levi, which was one of the twelve tribes of Israel. The Levite priests ministered before God first at the Tabernacle during the journey through the desert, then at the Temple in

Jerusalem. The priests offered bloody sacrifices for the sins of the people.

Of all the Levite priests, only the High Priest was allowed to enter the Holy of Holies. That is the place in the Tabernacle and Temple where the presence of God was manifested and the Ark of the Covenant was kept. The Ark represented the Holiness of God and was a symbol of God's covenant with Israel. The High Priest, who was appointed by God, acted as mediator between the people and Jehovah. Once a year, the High Priest entered the Holy of Holies to intercede with God on behalf of the nation of Israel. Before he could do this, he first had to make an offering for his own sins. His office ended with his death.

The Levite priesthood was imperfect and temporary. Countless blood sacrifices were offered for the sins of the people, but they could not remove the stain of sin from the people or satisfy God's price for sin. The Levite priesthood only foreshadowed Christ's eternal priesthood. It symbolized that which was to come which is the eternal High Priest office of Christ our Lord. Christ offered the perfect sacrifice — His own life — which completely and finally atoned for the sins of man. Christ our High Priest has past through the heavenlies to the right hand of the Father where He now ministers on behalf of believers (Hebrews 7:21-28; 8:1).

Hebrews 7:21-28

"(For those priests were made without an oath; but this with an oath by him that said unto him, The Lord sware and will not repent, Thou art a priest for ever after the order of Melchizedek:) By so much was Jesus made a surety of a better testament. And they truly were many priests, because they were not suffered to continue by reason of death: But

this man, because he continueth ever, hath an unchangeable priesthood. Wherefore he is able also to save them to the uttermost that come unto God by him, seeing he ever liveth to make intercession for them. For such an high priest became us, who is holy, harmless, undefiled, separate from sinners, and made higher than the heavens; Who needeth not daily, as those high priests, to offer up sacrifice, first for his own sins, and then for the people's: for this he did once, when he offered up himself. For the law maketh men high priests which have infirmity; but the word of the oath, which was since the law, maketh the Son, who is consecrated for evermore."

<u>Hebrews 8:1</u>

"Now of the things which we have spoken this is the sum: We have such an high priest, who is set on the right hand of the throne of the Majesty in the heavens."

<u>Hebrews 6:20</u>

"Whither the forerunner is for us entered, even Jesus, made an high priest for ever after the order of Melchizedek."

REVIEW

The priests were descendants of which tribe?

The priests were descendants of the tribe of Levi.

What does the Ark of the Covenant symbolize?

It symbolizes the Holiness of God and God's covenant with Israel.

What is the extent of the High Priest office of our Lord Christ Jesus?

Our Lord Christ is our eternal High Priest.

Why can Christ our High Priest sympathize with our weaknesses?

Because He was tempted in all points as we are, yet He did not sin.

---

5. The Anointed King

   Luke 1:32-33

   "He shall be great, and shall be called the Son of the Highest: and the Lord God shall give unto him the throne of his father David: And he shall reign over the house of Jacob for ever; and of his kingdom there shall be no end."

   Psalm 2:6-7

   "Yet have I set my king upon my holy hill of Zion. I will declare the decree: the Lord hath said unto me, Thou art my Son; this day have I begotten thee."

Psalm 45:6-7

"Thy throne, O God, is for ever and ever: the scepter of thy kingdom is a right scepter. Thou lovest righteousness, and hatest wickedness: therefore God, thy God, hath anointed thee with the oil of gladness above thy fellows."

Saul was Israel's first king. He was chosen because the people rejected God's lordship over them. They wanted to be like the other nations. God promised Saul great blessings if he would obey and serve Him. However, Saul failed to obey God and was rejected by Him (1 Sam.15:22-23). God then chose David to be king over Israel because his heart was right with Him (1Sam. 16:1; 1 Sam. 16:13).

1 Samuel 15:22-23

"And Samuel said, Hath the Lord as great delight in burnt offerings and sacrifices, as in obeying the voice of the Lord? Behold, to obey is better than sacrifice, and to hearken than the fat of rams. For rebellion is as the sin of witchcraft, and stubbornness is as iniquity and idolatry. Because thou hast rejected the word of the Lord, he hath also rejected thee from being king."

1 Samuel 16:1

"And the Lord said unto Samuel, How long wilt thou mourn for Saul, seeing I have rejected him from reigning over Israel? fill thine horn with oil, and go, I will send thee to Jesse the

Bethlehemite: for I have provided me a king among his sons."

<u>1 Samuel 16:-12-13</u>

"And he sent, and brought him in. Now he was ruddy, and withal of a beautiful countenance, and goodly to look to. And the Lord said, Arise, anoint him: for this is he. Then Samuel took the horn of oil, and anointed him in the midst of his brethren: and the Spirit of the Lord came upon David from that day forward. So Samuel rose up, and went to Ramah."

God promised David a son whose kingdom would be everlasting. His kingdom would usher in an age of righteousness and blessing. Israel would be especially blessed above all nations. David later fell into great sin, but God did not remove His promises to him. They would be fulfilled in Christ Jesus who is of David's line. Christ is the One whom God would install as king over an everlasting kingdom of peace and righteousness (Jer. 23:5-6).

<u>Jeremiah 23:5-6</u>

"Behold, the days come, saith the Lord, that I will raise unto David a righteous Branch, and a King shall reign and prosper, and shall execute judgment and justice in the earth. In his days Judah shall be saved, and Israel shall dwell safely: and this is his name whereby he shall be called, THE LORD OUR RIGHTEOUSNESS."

Isaiah 9:6-7

"For unto us a child is born, unto us a son is given: and the government shall be upon his shoulder: and his name shall be called Wonderful, Counselor, The mighty God, The everlasting Father, The Prince of Peace. Of the increase of his government and peace there shall be no end, upon the throne of David, and upon his kingdom, to order it, and to establish it with judgment and with justice from henceforth even for ever. The zeal of the Lord of hosts will perform this."

Revelation 19:16

"And he hath on his vesture and on his thigh a name written, KING OF KINGS, AND LORD OF LORDS."

REVIEW

Who was Israel's first king?

The first king of Israel was Saul. He was the people's choice.

Who was God's appointed King to Israel?

God chose David to be king over Israel.

What kingship did David represent?

David's kingdom was a foreshadowing of the kingdom of Christ our Lord.

How long will the kingdom of Christ our Lord last?

The kingdom of Christ will last for all eternity.

What is the meaning of the name "Christ"?

The name Christ means "Anointed One."

---

6. Messiah

John 1:41

> "He first findeth his own brother Simon, and saith unto him, We have found the Messiah, which is, being interpreted, the Christ."
> This word means "Christ" or "Anointed One." Messiah is the name given to the One who would usher in the everlasting kingdom and deliver Israel from the hand of her enemies.

Daniel 9:25-26

> "Know therefore and understand, that from the going forth of the commandment to restore and to build Jerusalem unto the Messiah the Prince shall be seven weeks, and threescore and two weeks: the street shall be built again, and the wall, even in troublous times. And

after threescore and two weeks shall Messiah be cut off, but not for himself: and the people of the prince that shall come shall destroy the city and the sanctuary; and the end thereof shall be with a flood, and unto the end of the war desolations are determined."

John 4:25-26

"The woman saith unto him, I know that Messiah cometh, which is called Christ: when he is come, he will tell us all things. Jesus saith unto her, I that speak unto thee am he."

7. Lord

Romans 10:9, 13

"That if thou shalt confess with thy mouth the Lord Jesus, and shalt believe in thine heart that God hath raised him from the dead, thou shalt be saved." "For whosoever shall call upon the name of the LORD shall be saved."

This name reveals to us that Jesus is indeed God. This verse quotes an Old Testament Scripture (Joel 2:32) and identifies Jesus as the name of God on which people call for salvation.

Joel 2:32

"And it shall come to pass, that whosoever shall call on the name of the LORD shall be delivered: for in mount Zion and in Jerusalem shall be deliverance, as the LORD hath said,

and in the remnant whom the LORD shall call."

8. Son of God

Luke 1:35

"And the angel answered and said unto her, The Holy Ghost shall come upon thee, and the power of the Highest shall overshadow thee: therefore also that holy thing which shall be born of thee shall be called the Son of God."

This title reflects the supernatural beginning of Christ's human existence. He was born of a virgin, having been miraculously conceived by God. It shows His glory as the only begotten Son of God.

John 3:18

"He that believeth on him is not condemned: but he that believeth not is condemned already, because he hath not believed in the name of the only begotten Son of God."

John 11:27

"She saith unto him, Yea, Lord: I believe that thou art the Christ, the Son of God, which should come into the world."

1 John 3:8

"He that committeth sin is of the devil; for the devil sinneth from the beginning. For this

purpose the Son of God was manifested, that he might destroy the works of the devil."

1 John 4:15

"Whosoever shall confess that Jesus is the Son of God, God dwelleth in him, and he in God."

1 John 5:10-12

"He that believeth on the Son of God hath the witness in himself: he that believeth not God hath made him a liar; because he believeth not the record that God gave of his Son. And this is the record, that God hath given to us eternal life, and this life is in his Son. He that hath the Son hath life; and he that hath not the Son of God hath not life."

1 John 5:13

"These things have I written unto you that believe on the name of the Son of God; that ye may know that ye have eternal life, and that ye may believe on the name of the Son of God."

1 John 5:20

"And we know that the Son of God is come, and hath given us an understanding, that we may know him that is true, and we are in him that is true, even in his Son Jesus Christ. This is the true God, and eternal life."

9. Son of Abraham

   Galatians 3:16

   "Now to Abraham and his seed were the promises made. He saith not, And to seeds, as of many; but as of one, And to thy seed, which is Christ."

   Matthew 1:1

   "The book of the generation of Jesus Christ, the son of David, the son of Abraham."

This title supports the fact that He is the Messiah. God made a covenant with Abraham (Gen. 12; 22:18) that his seed will provide spiritual blessings to the whole world. Galatians 3:16 identifies this Seed as Christ.

   Genesis 22:18

   "And in thy seed shall all the nations of the earth be blessed; because thou hast obeyed my voice."

   Galatians 3:16

   "Now to Abraham and his seed were the promises made. He saith not, And to seeds, as of many; but as of one, And to thy seed, which is Christ."

10. Son of David

Matthew 1:1

"The book of the generation of Jesus Christ, the son of David, the Son of Abraham."

Matthew 9:27

"And when Jesus departed thence, two blind men followed him, crying, and saying, Thou Son of David, have mercy on us."

Mark 10:46-47

"And they came to Jericho: and as he went out of Jericho with his disciples and a great number of people, blind Bartimaeus, the son of Timaeus, sat by the highway side begging. And when he heard that it was Jesus of Nazareth, he began to cry out, and say, Jesus, thou Son of David, have mercy on me."

This title shows His royalty. David was God's chosen King for Israel. He represented the eternal kingship of Christ Jesus our Lord.

2 Samuel 7:12-13

"And when thy days be fulfilled, and thou shalt sleep with thy fathers, I will set up thy seed after thee, which shall proceed out of thy bowels, and I will establish his kingdom. He shall build an house for my name, and I will establish the throne of his kingdom for ever."

Psalm 89:3-4

"I have made a covenant with my chosen, I have sworn unto David my servant, Thy seed will I establish for ever, and build up thy throne to all generations."

Psalm 132:11

"The Lord hath sworn in truth unto David; he will not turn from it; Of the fruit of thy body will I set upon thy throne."

Matthew 15:22

"And, behold, a woman of Canaan came out of the same coasts, and cried unto him, saying, Have mercy on me, O Lord, thou Son of David; my daughter is grievously vexed with a devil."

Matthew 21:9

"And the multitudes that went before, and that followed, cried, saying, Hosanna to the Son of David: Blessed is he that cometh in the name of the Lord; Hosanna in the highest."

Matthew 22:41-42

"While the Pharisees were gathered together, Jesus asked them, Saying, What think ye of Christ? whose son is he? They say unto him, The Son of David."

Romans 1:3-4

"Concerning his Son Jesus Christ our Lord, which was made of the seed of David according to the flesh; And declared to be the Son of God with power, according to the Spirit of holiness, by the resurrection from the dead."

11. Son of the Highest

Luke 1:32-33

"He shall be great, and shall be called the Son of the Highest: and the Lord God shall give unto him the throne of his father David: And he shall reign over the house of Jacob for ever; and of his kingdom there shall be no end."

This title reveals His preeminence as the only begotten Son of God. It declares Him as King. He reigns from on high. His kingdom is eternal.

Mark 5:7

"And cried with a loud voice, and said, What have I to do with thee, Jesus, thou Son of the most high God? I adjure thee by God, that thou torment me not."

12. Last Adam

1 Corinthians 15:22

"For as in Adam all die, even so in Christ shall all be made alive."

1 Corinthians 15:45

"And so it is written, The first man Adam was made a living soul; the last Adam was made a quickening spirit."

This title reveals the victory He won over sin and death. The first man Adam brought sin and consequently spiritual death. All men are of Adam by the natural birth and are under sin. The last Adam, who is Christ, was made a quickening spirit. That is, He won the victory over sin and death (Rom. 5:12-21).

Romans 5:12-21

"Wherefore, as by one man sin entered into the world, and death by sin; and so death passed upon all men, for that all have sinned: (For until the law sin was in the world: but sin is not imputed when there is no law. Nevertheless death reigned from Adam to Moses, even over them that had not sinned after the similitude of Adam's transgression, who is the figure of him that was to come. But not as the offense, so also is the free gift. For if through the offense of one many be dead, much more the grace of God, and the gift by grace, which is by one man, Jesus Christ,

hath abounded unto many. And not as it was by one that sinned, so is the gift: for the judgment was by one to condemnation, but the free gift is of many offenses unto justification. For if by one man's offense death reigned by one; much more they which receive abundance of grace and of the gift of righteousness shall reign in life by one, Jesus Christ.) Therefore as by the offense of one judgment came upon all men to condemnation; even so by the righteousness of one the free gift came upon all men unto justification of life. For as by one man's disobedience many were made sinners, so by the obedience of one shall many be made righteous. Moreover the law entered, that the offense might abound. But where sin abounded, grace did much more abound: That as sin hath reigned unto death, even so might grace reign through righteousness unto eternal life by Jesus Christ our Lord."

13. Emmanuel

Isaiah 7:14

"Therefore the Lord himself shall give you a sign; Behold, a virgin shall conceive, and bear a son, and shall call his name Immanuel."

Matthew 1:23

"Behold, a virgin shall be with child, and shall bring forth a son, and they shall call his name Immanuel, which being interpreted is, God with us."

This name means "God with us." Our Lord Christ Jesus is God. He came in the form of flesh to die on the cross for the sin of mankind (Philip. 2:5-11).

Philippians 2:5-11

"Let this mind be in you, which was also in Christ Jesus: Who, being in the form of God, thought it not robbery to be equal with God: But made himself of no reputation, and took upon him the form of a servant, and was made in the likeness of men: And being found in fashion as a man, he humbled himself, and became obedient unto death, even the death of the cross. Wherefore God also hath highly exalted him, and given him a name which is above every name: That at the name of Jesus every knee should bow, of things in heaven, and things in earth, and things under the earth; And that every tongue should confess that Jesus Christ is Lord, to the glory of God the Father."

14. Savior

Luke 2:11

"For unto you is born this day in the city of David a Savior, which is Christ the Lord."

This title refers to our Lord Christ Jesus as our deliverer and preserver. Jesus' death on the cross paid for all our sins and saved us from God's wrath.

2 Timothy 1:9-10

"Who hath saved us, and called us with an holy calling, not according to our works, but according to his own purpose and grace, which was given us in Christ Jesus before the world began, But is now made manifest by the appearing of our Savior Jesus Christ, who hath abolished death, and hath brought life and immortality to light through the Gospel."

Titus 2:11-14

"For the grace of God that bringeth salvation hath appeared to all men, Teaching us that, denying ungodliness and worldly lusts, we should live soberly, righteously, and godly, in this present world; Looking for that blessed hope, and the glorious appearing of the great God and our Savior Jesus Christ; Who gave himself for us, that he might redeem us from all iniquity, and purify unto himself a peculiar people, zealous of good works."

Hebrews 7:25

"Wherefore he is able also to save them to the uttermost that come unto God by him, seeing he ever liveth to make intercession for them."

Hebrews 9:24

"For Christ is not entered into the holy places made with hands, which are the figures of the

true; but into heaven itself, now to appear in the presence of God for us:"

1 John 2:2

"And he is the propitiation for our sins: and not for ours only, but also for the sins of the whole world."

15. The Word

John 1:1

"In the beginning was the word, and the word was with God, and the word was God."

This title means that Christ Jesus who is the living Word is revealing the invisible God.

John 1:14

"And the word was made flesh, and dwelt among us, (and we beheld his glory, the glory as of the only begotten of the Father) full of grace and truth."

Revelation 19:11-13

"And I saw heaven opened, and behold a white horse; and he that sat upon him was called Faithful and True, and in righteousness he doth judge and make war… and his name is called The Word of God."

REVIEW

What does the title "Son of Abraham" teach us?

It declares the humanity of Christ, the fact that He was a Jew and descendant of Abraham.

What does the title "Son of David" teach us?

It reveals the royalty of our Lord Christ Jesus.

What is the meaning of the title "The Son of the Highest"?

It means that He is the eternal King who reigns over all.

What is the meaning of the word "Emmanuel"?

It means, "God with us."

What is the meaning of the title "the Last Adam"?

This reveals the victory which Christ has won. While the first Adam brought spiritual defeat, the Last Adam (Christ Jesus) brought spiritual victory.

What is the meaning of the title "Savior"?

Through His death, burial and resurrection, Jesus has provided the means whereby anyone can be saved for all eternity. This salvation has to be received by faith.

Who is the "Word"?

Our Lord Christ Jesus is the Word.

---

16. The Son

The title "Son" teaches us of our Lord Jesus Christ's eternal existence. He is both Creator and Heir of all things. He is the perfect image of God, because He is God. He existed in eternity past and was sent by God the Father to redeem mankind from his sins. "For unto us a child is born, unto us a Son is given" (Isa. 9:6; Matt. 1:21).

<u>Isaiah 9:6</u>

"For unto us a child is born, unto us a son is given..."

<u>Matthew 1:21</u>

"And she shall bring forth a son, and thou shalt call his name Jesus: for he shall save his people from their sins."

<u>John 3:16-17</u>

"For God so loved the world, that he gave his only begotten Son, that whosoever believeth in him should not perish, but have everlasting life. For God sent not his Son into the world to condemn the world; but that the world through him might be saved."

Psalm 2:7

"I will declare the decree: the Lord hath said unto me, Thou art my Son; this day have I begotten thee."

John 1:18

"No man hath seen God at any time; the only begotten Son, which is in the bosom of the Father, he hath declared him."

Hebrews 5:5

"So also Christ glorified not himself to be made an high priest; but he that said unto him, Thou art my Son, to day have I begotten thee."

1 John 4:9-10

"In this was manifested the love of God toward us, because that God sent his only begotten Son into the world, that we might live through him. Herein is love, not that we loved God, but that he loved us, and sent his Son to be the propitiation for our sins."

17. Son of Man

"Son of man" is the title that our Lord Jesus Christ applied to Himself. This title is recorded more than 50 times in the four gospels. This is a messianic title that teaches that the Lord Jesus Christ sits at the right hand of God as both fully God and fully man. He is the Lord from heaven who came to earth as mankind's representative to fulfill the will of the Father. The Father's will for the Son of man was to give his life a ransom for many (Mark 10:45; Mark 8:31; Matt. 26:2; Matt. 26:24).

Mark 10:45

"For even the Son of man came not to be ministered unto, but to minister, and to give his life a ransom for many."

Mark 8:31

"And he began to teach them, that the Son of man must suffer many things, and be rejected of the elders, and of the chief priests, and scribes, and be killed, and after three days rise again."

Matthew 26:2

"Ye know that after two days is the feast of the Passover, and the Son of man is betrayed to be crucified."

Matthew 26:24

"The Son of man goeth as it is written of him: but woe unto that man by whom the Son of man is betrayed! it had been good for that man if he had not been born."

Daniel 7:13-14

"I saw in the night visions, and, behold, one like the Son of man came with the clouds of heaven, and came to the Ancient of days, and they brought him near before him. And there was given him dominion, and glory, and a kingdom, that all people, nations, and languages, should serve him: his dominion is an everlasting dominion, which shall not pass away, and his kingdom that which shall not be destroyed."

Luke 19:10

"For the Son of man is come to seek and to save that which was lost."

Matthew 9:6

"But that ye may know that the Son of man hath power on earth to forgive sins, (then saith he to the sick of the palsy,) 'Arise, take up thy bed, and go unto thine house.'"

Matthew 16:27

"For the Son of man shall come in the glory of his Father with his angels; and then he shall reward every man according to his works."

Matthew 24:27

"For as the lightning cometh out of the east, and shineth even unto the west; so shall also the coming of the Son of man be."

Matthew 24:30

"And then shall appear the sign of the Son of man in heaven: and then shall all the tribes of the earth mourn, and they shall see the Son of man coming in the clouds of heaven with power and great glory."

Matthew 24:37

"But as the days of Noah were, so shall also the coming of the Son of man be."

Matthew 24:44

"Therefore be ye also ready: for in such an hour as ye think not the Son of man cometh."

Matthew 25:13

"Watch therefore, for ye know neither the day nor the hour wherein the Son of man cometh."

Matthew 25:31

"When the Son of man shall come in his glory, and all the holy angels with him, then shall he sit upon the throne of his glory:"

Matthew 26:64

"Jesus saith unto him, Thou hast said: nevertheless I say unto you, Hereafter shall ye see the Son of man sitting on the right hand of power, and coming in the clouds of heaven."

Mark 8:38

"Whosoever therefore shall be ashamed of me and of my words in this adulterous and sinful generation; of him also shall the Son of man be ashamed, when he cometh in the glory of his Father with the holy angels."

Mark 9:9

"And as they came down from the mountain, he charged them that they should tell no man what things they had seen, till the Son of man were risen from the dead."

Mark 9:12

"And he answered and told them, Elijah verily cometh first, and restoreth all things; and how it is written of the Son of man, that he must suffer many things, and be set at nought."

Mark 9:31

"For he taught his disciples, and said unto them, The Son of man is delivered into the hands of men, and they shall kill him; and

after that he is killed, he shall rise the third day."

<u>Mark 13:26</u>

"And then shall they see the Son of man coming in the clouds with great power and glory."

<u>Mark 14:21</u>

"The Son of man indeed goeth, as it is written of him: but woe to that man by whom the Son of man is betrayed! good were it for that man if he had never been born."

<u>Mark 14:41</u>

"And he cometh the third time, and saith unto them, Sleep on now, and take your rest: it is enough, the hour is come; behold, the Son of man is betrayed into the hands of sinners."

<u>Mark 14:62</u>

"And Jesus said, I am: and ye shall see the Son of man sitting on the right hand of power, and coming in the clouds of heaven."

<u>Luke 9:56</u>

"For the Son of man is not come to destroy men's lives, but to save them...."

Luke 9:58

"And Jesus said unto him, Foxes have holes, and birds of the air have nests; but the Son of man hath not where to lay his head."

Luke 12:40

"Be ye therefore ready also: for the Son of man cometh at an hour when ye think not."

Luke 17:22

"And he said unto the disciples, The days will come, when ye shall desire to see one of the days of the Son of man, and ye shall not see it."

Luke 17:24

"For as the lightning, that lighteneth out of the one part under heaven, shineth unto the other part under heaven; so shall also the Son of man be in his day. "

Luke 17:26-30

"And as it was in the days of Noah, so shall it be also in the days of the Son of man. They did eat, they drank, they married wives, they were given in marriage, until the day that Noah entered into the ark, and the flood came, and destroyed them all. Likewise also as it was in the days of Lot; they did eat, they drank, they bought, they sold, they planted, they builded;

But the same day that Lot went out of Sodom it rained fire and brimstone from heaven, and destroyed them all. Even thus shall it be in the day when the Son of man is revealed."

<u>Luke 18:8</u>

"I tell you that he will avenge them speedily. Nevertheless when the Son of man cometh, shall he find faith on the earth?"

<u>Luke 18:31</u>

"Then he took unto him the twelve, and said unto them, Behold, we go up to Jerusalem, and all things that are written by the prophets concerning the Son of man shall be accomplished."

<u>Luke 21:27</u>

"And then shall they see the Son of man coming in a cloud with power and great glory."

<u>Luke 21:36</u>

"Watch ye therefore, and pray always, that ye may be accounted worthy to escape all these things that shall come to pass, and to stand before the Son of man."

Luke 22:22

"And truly the Son of man goeth, as it was determined: but woe unto that man by whom he is betrayed!"

Luke 22:48

"But Jesus said unto him, Judas, betrayest thou the Son of man with a kiss?"

Luke 22:69

"Hereafter shall the Son of man sit on the right hand of the power of God."

Luke 24:6-7

"He is not here, but is risen: remember how he spake unto you when he was yet in Galilee, Saying, The Son of man must be delivered into the hands of sinful men, and be crucified, and the third day rise again."

John 1:51

"And he saith unto him, Verily, verily, I say unto you, Hereafter ye shall see heaven open, and the angels of God ascending and descending upon the Son of man."

John 3:13-15

"And no man hath ascended up to heaven, but he that came down from heaven, even the Son *of man which is in heaven. And as Moses lifted up the serpent in the wilderness, even so must the Son of man be lifted up: That whosoever believeth in him should not perish, but have eternal life.*

<u>John 5:27</u>

"And hath given him authority to execute judgment also, because he is the Son of man."

<u>John 6:27</u>

"Labor not for the meat which perisheth, but for that meat which endureth unto everlasting life, which the Son of man shall give unto you: for him hath God the Father sealed."

<u>John 6:53</u>

"Then Jesus said unto them, Verily, verily, I say unto you, Except ye eat the flesh of the Son of man, and drink his blood, ye have no life in you."

<u>John 6:62</u>

"What and if ye shall see the Son of man ascend up where he was before?"

<u>John 8:28</u>

"Then said Jesus unto them, When ye have lifted up the Son of man, then shall ye know that I am he, and that I do nothing of myself;

but as my Father hath taught me, I speak these things."

John 12:23

"And Jesus answered them, saying, The hour is come, that the Son of man should be glorified."

John 12:34

"The people answered him, We have heard out of the law that Christ abideth for ever: and how sayest thou, The Son of man must be lifted up? who is this Son of man?"

John 13:31

"Therefore, when he was gone out, Jesus said, Now is the Son of man glorified, and God is glorified in him."

Acts 7:55-56

"But he, being full of the Holy Ghost, looked up steadfastly into heaven, and saw the glory of God, and Jesus standing on the right hand of God, And said, Behold, I see the heavens opened, and the Son of man standing on the right hand of God."

Revelation 1:13-16

"And in the midst of the seven candlesticks one like unto the Son of man, clothed with a *garment down to the foot, and girt about the paps with a golden girdle. His head and his hairs were white like wool, as white as snow; and his eyes were as a flame of fire; And his feet like unto fine brass, as if they burned in a furnace; and his voice as the sound of many waters. And he had in his right hand seven stars: and out of his mouth went a sharp two-edged sword: and his countenance was as the sun shineth in his strength."*

<u>Revelation 14:14</u>

"And I looked, and behold a white cloud, and upon the cloud one sat like unto the Son of man, having on his head a golden crown, and in his hand a sharp sickle."

18. Lamb of God

<u>John 1:29</u>

"The next day John seeth Jesus coming unto him, and saith, Behold the Lamb of God, which taketh away the sin of the world."

<u>John 1:36</u>

"And looking upon Jesus as he walked, he saith, Behold the Lamb of God!"

<u>1 Peter 1:19-20</u>

"But with the precious blood of Christ, as of a lamb without blemish and without spot: Who

> *verily was foreordained before the foundation of the world, but was manifest in these last times for you."*

In the Old Testament, the lamb was used for a sacrifice at the Passover (Ex.12) and the sin offering (Lev. 4). It was a foreshadowing of the Lord Jesus Christ who would serve as God's sinless lamb to take away the sin of the world. Our Lord Jesus was the One sent by God to suffer and to become the sacrificial lamb for the sin of the world (1 John 2:2). By the blood of the Lamb of God, the sins of the people have been purged and they have been reconciled with God.

1 John 2:2

> *"And He is the propitiation for our sins; and not for ours only, but also for the sins of the whole world"*

Isaiah prophesied of the lamb of God, the Lord Jesus Christ, who was sacrificed for the transgression of the people (Isaiah 53:5-12).

Isaiah 53:5-12

> *"But he was wounded for our transgressions, he was bruised for our iniquities: the chastisement of our peace was upon him; and with his stripes we are healed. All we like sheep have gone astray; we have turned every one to his own way; and the Lord hath laid on him the iniquity of us all. He was oppressed, and he was afflicted, yet he opened not his mouth: he is brought as a lamb to the slaughter, and as a sheep before her shearers is dumb, so*

he openeth not his mouth. He was taken from prison and from judgment: and who shall declare his generation? for he was cut off out of the land of the living: for the transgression of my people was he stricken. And he made his grave with the wicked, and with the rich in his death; because he had done no violence, neither was any deceit in his mouth.

Yet it pleased the Lord to bruise him; he hath put him to grief: when thou shalt make his soul an offering for sin, he shall see his seed, he shall prolong his days, and the pleasure of the Lord shall prosper in his hand. He shall see of the travail of his soul, and shall be satisfied: by his knowledge shall my righteous servant justify many; for he shall bear their iniquities. Therefore will I divide him a portion with the great, and he shall divide the spoil with the strong; because he hath poured out his soul unto death: and he was numbered with the transgressors; and he bare the sin of many, and made intercession for the transgressors."

<u>Acts 8:32</u>

"The place of the Scripture which he read was this, He was led as a sheep to the slaughter; and like a lamb dumb before his shearer, so opened he not his mouth."

<u>Revelation 5:6-14</u>

"And I beheld, and, lo, in the midst of the throne and of the four beasts, and in the midst *of the elders, stood a Lamb as it had been slain, having seven horns and seven eyes, which are the seven Spirits of God sent forth into all the earth. And he came and took the book out of the right hand of him that sat upon the throne. And when he had taken the book, the four beasts and four and twenty elders fell down before the Lamb, having every one of them harps, and golden vials full of odors, which are the prayers of saints. And they sung a new song, saying, Thou art worthy to take the book, and to open the seals thereof: for thou wast slain, and hast redeemed us to God by thy blood out of every kindred, and tongue, and people, and nation; And hast made us unto our God kings and priests: and we shall reign on the earth. And I beheld, and I heard the voice of many angels round about the throne and the beasts and the elders: and the number of them was ten thousand times ten thousand, and thousands of thousands; Saying with a loud voice, Worthy is the Lamb that was slain to receive power, and riches, and wisdom, and strength, and honor, and glory, and blessing. And every creature which is in heaven, and on the earth, and under the earth, and such as are in the sea, and all that are in them, heard I saying, Blessing, and honor, and glory, and power, be unto him that sitteth upon the throne, and unto the Lamb for ever and ever. And the four beasts said, Amen. And the four and twenty elders fell down and worshipped him that liveth for ever and ever."*

Revelation. 6:1

"And I saw when the Lamb opened one of the seals, and I heard, as it were the noise of thunder, one of the four beasts saying, Come and see."

Revelation 17:14

"These shall make war with the Lamb, and the Lamb shall overcome them: for he is Lord of lords, and King of kings: and they that are with him are called, and chosen, and faithful."

19. Shepherd

John 10:11

"I am the good Shepherd: the good Shepherd giveth his life for the sheep."

John 10:14-18

"I am the good shepherd, and know my sheep, and am known of mine. As the Father knoweth me, even so know I the Father: and I lay down my life for the sheep. And other sheep I have, which are not of this fold: them also I must bring, and they shall hear my voice; and there shall be one fold, and one shepherd. Therefore doth my Father love me, because I lay down my life, that I might take it again. No man taketh it from me, but I lay it down of myself. I have power to lay it down, and I have power

> *to take it again. This commandment have I received of my Father."*

The image of the Lord as Shepherd is illustrated frequently in the Old and New Testaments. God's people are never pictured in Scripture as mighty independent, self-sufficient people. They are pictured as sheep that have gone astray and are in need of a Shepherd to lead them and to save them. God expects them to be totally dependent on their Shepherd for salvation, provision, protection and guidance.

When the Lord Jesus Christ described Himself as the "Good Shepherd," He was claiming to be God. This term expresses the Lord Jesus' role as the Savior, protector and provider for His people. Christ Jesus is illustrated as the Shepherd and believers are His sheep. Mankind is described in Scripture as sheep who have all gone astray (Isaiah 53:6; 1 Peter 2:25). He is totally depraved and is appointed to suffer the wrath of God (Gen. 6:5; John 3:36). Christ Jesus is the Shepherd who was appointed to propitiate the wrath of God for His people by giving his life for the sheep (John 10:11).

> *Isaiah 53:6*
>
> *"All we like sheep have gone astray; we have turned every one to his own way; and the Lord hath laid on him the iniquity of us all."*
>
> *1 Peter 2:25*
>
> *"For ye were as sheep going astray; but are now returned unto the Shepherd and Bishop of your souls."*

Genesis 6:5

"And God saw that the wickedness of man was great in the earth, and that every imagination of the thoughts of his heart was only evil continually."

John 3:36

"He that believeth on the Son hath everlasting life: and he that believeth not the Son shall not see life; but the wrath of God abideth on him."

John 10:27-30

"My sheep hear my voice, and I know them, and they follow me: And I give unto them eternal life; and they shall never perish, neither shall any man pluck them out of my hand. My Father, which gave them me, is greater than all; and no man is able to pluck them out of my Father's hand. I and my Father are one."

Mark 14:27-28

"And Jesus saith unto them, All ye shall be offended because of me this night: for it is written, 'I will smite the Shepherd, and the sheep shall be scattered.' But after that I am risen, I will go before you into Galilee."

Isaiah 40:11

"He shall feed his flock like a shepherd: he shall gather the lambs with his arm, and carry them in his bosom, and shall gently lead those that are with young."

Jeremiah 31:10

"Hear the word of the Lord, O ye nations, and declare it in the isles afar off, and say, He that scattered Israel will gather him, and keep him, as a shepherd doth his flock."

1 Peter 5:4

"And when the chief Shepherd shall appear, ye shall receive a crown of glory that fadeth not away."

Hebrews 13:20-21

"Now the God of peace, that brought again from the dead our Lord Jesus, that great Shepherd of the sheep, through the blood of the everlasting covenant, Make you perfect in every good work to do his will, working in you that which is well-pleasing in his sight, through Jesus Christ; to whom be glory for ever and ever. Amen."

Psalm 23:1

"The Lord is my shepherd; I shall not want."

Ezekiel 34:22-24

"Therefore will I save my flock, and they shall no more be a prey; and I will judge between cattle and cattle. And I will set up one shepherd over them, and he shall feed them, even my servant David; he shall feed them, and he shall be their shepherd. And I the Lord will be their God, and my servant David a prince among them; I the Lord have spoken it."

20. King of Kings

Revelation 19:16

"And he hath on his vesture and on his thigh a name written, KING OF KINGS, AND LORD OF LORDS."

Psalm 2:6-7

"Yet have I set my king upon my holy hill of Zion. I will declare the decree: the Lord hath said unto me, 'Thou art my Son; this day have I begotten thee.'"

God the Father promised to set up a King whose kingdom would be an everlasting kingdom. Our Lord Jesus Christ is God's anointed King who sits upon the throne of His Father David. The Lord said to David through Prophet Nathan that he would build a house for His name's sake and would establish His kingdom forever (2 Sam. 7:12-13). Our Lord Jesus Christ is the eternal King who will ultimately reign over all earthly kings.

2 Samuel 7:12-13

"And when thy days be fulfilled, and thou shalt sleep with thy fathers, I will set up thy seed after thee, which shall proceed out of thy bowels, and I will establish his kingdom. He shall build an house for my name, and I will stablish the throne of his kingdom for ever."

1 Chronicles 17:11-15

"And it shall come to pass, when thy days be expired that thou must go to be with thy fathers, that I will raise up thy seed after thee, which shall be of thy sons; and I will establish his kingdom. He shall build me an house, and I will establish his throne for ever. I will be his father, and he shall be my son: and I will not take my mercy away from him, as I took it from him that was before thee: But I will settle him in mine house and in my kingdom for ever: and his throne shall be established for evermore. According to all these words, and according to all this vision, so did Nathan speak unto David."

Revelation 17:14

"These shall make war with the Lamb, and the Lamb shall overcome them: for he is Lord of lords, and King of kings: and they that are with him are called, and chosen, and faithful."

1 Timothy 6:15

"Which in his times he shall show, who is the blessed and only Potentate, the King of kings, and Lord of lords."

21. Lord of Lords

Revelation 19:16

"And he hath on his vesture and on his thigh a name written, KING OF KINGS, AND LORD OF LORDS."

Scripture reveals that our Lord Jesus Christ is the Lord of lords. There are many lords in the earth, but there is only one Lord who will rule over all and that is the Lord Jesus Christ.

Revelation 17:14

"These shall make war with the Lamb, and the Lamb shall overcome them: for he is Lord of lords, and King of kings: and they that are with him are called, and chosen, and faithful."

1 Timothy 6:15

"Which in his times he shall show, who is the blessed and only Potentate, the King of kings, and Lord of lords."

22. The Righteous Judge

2 Timothy 4:8

"Henceforth there is laid up for me a crown of righteousness, which the Lord, the righteous judge, shall give me at that day: and not to me only, but unto all them also that love his appearing."

John 5:22

"For the Father judgeth no man, but hath committed all judgment unto the Son."

Our Lord Christ Jesus is the Righteous Judge before whom all men must appear, whether believers or unbelievers. The believers will appear before the judgment seat of Christ to receive rewards for their obedience and service to Him (Rom.14:10-12; 1 Cor. 3:8-15; 4:5; Rev. 22:12). However, in contrast unbelievers must appear before the Great White Throne judgment to be condemned for their rejection of the Lord Jesus Christ. Their final destination will be the Lake of Fire (Rev. 20:11-15).

Romans 14:10-12

"But why dost thou judge thy brother? or why dost thou set at nought thy brother? for we shall all stand before the judgment seat of Christ. For it is written, As I live, saith the Lord, every knee shall bow to me, and every tongue shall confess to God. So then every one of us shall give account of himself to God."

1 Corinthians 3:8-15

"Now he that planteth and he that watereth are one: and every man shall receive his own reward according to his own labor. For we are laborers together with God: ye are God's husbandry, ye are God's building. According to the grace of God which is given unto me, as a wise masterbuilder, I have laid the foundation, and another buildeth thereon. But let every man take heed how he buildeth thereupon. For other foundation can no man lay than that is laid, which is Jesus Christ. Now if any man build upon this foundation gold, silver, precious stones, wood, hay, stubble; Every man's work shall be made manifest: for the day shall declare it, because it shall be revealed by fire; and the fire shall try every man's work of what sort it is. If any man's work abide which he hath built thereupon, he shall receive a reward. If any man's work shall be burned, he shall suffer loss: but he himself shall be saved; yet so as by fire."

1 Corinthians 4:5

"Therefore judge nothing before the time, until the Lord come, who both will bring to light the hidden things of darkness, and will make manifest the counsels of the hearts: and then shall every man have praise of God."

Revelation 22:12

"And, behold, I come quickly; and my reward is with me, to give every man according as his work shall be."

Revelation 20:11-15

"And I saw a great white throne, and him that sat on it, from whose face the earth and the heaven fled away; and there was found no place for them. And I saw the dead, small and great, stand before God; and the books were opened: and another book was opened, which is the Book of Life: and the dead were judged out of those things which were written in the books, according to their works. And the sea gave up the dead which were in it; and death and hell delivered up the dead which were in them: and they were judged every man according to their works. And death and hell were cast into the lake of fire. This is the second death. And whosoever was not found written in the Book of Life was cast into the lake of fire.

John 5:27

"And hath given him authority to execute judgment also, because he is the Son of man."

Acts 10:42

"And he commanded us to preach unto the people, and to testify that it is he which was ordained of God to be the Judge of quick and dead."

Acts 17:31

"Because he hath appointed a day, in the which he will judge the world in righteousness by that man whom he hath ordained; whereof he hath given assurance unto all men, in that he hath raised him from the dead."

Romans 2:16

"In the day when God shall judge the secrets of men by Jesus Christ according to my gospel."

Psalm 9:7-8

"But the Lord shall endure for ever: he hath prepared his throne for judgment. And he shall judge the world in righteousness, he shall minister judgment to the people in uprightness."

Jude 1:14-15

"And Enoch also, the seventh from Adam, prophesied of these, saying, Behold, the Lord cometh with ten thousands of his saints, To execute judgment upon all, and to convince all that are ungodly among them of all their ungodly deeds which they have ungodly committed, and of all their hard speeches which ungodly sinners have spoken against him."

Revelation 19:11

"And I saw heaven opened, and behold a white horse; and he that sat upon him was called Faithful and True, and in righteousness he doth judge and make war."

Revelation 19:15

"And out of his mouth goeth a sharp sword, that with it he should smite the nations: and he shall rule them with a rod of iron: and he treadeth the winepress of the fierceness and wrath of Almighty God."

23. Alpha and Omega

Revelation 1:8

"I am Alpha and Omega, the beginning and the ending, saith the Lord, which is, and which was, and which is to come, the Almighty."

Alpha and Omega, the first and last letters of the Greek alphabet, refers to Christ Jesus' eternality and sovereignty. It is recorded in Isaiah 44:6, "Thus saith the Lord the King of Israel, and his redeemer the Lord of hosts; I am the first, and I am the last; and beside me there is no God. In Revelation 22:13, Jesus said, "I am Alpha and Omega, the beginning and the end, the first and the last." Thus, Jesus' description of Himself is the same description of God revealed by Prophet Isaiah. Our Lord Christ Jesus is God. He is the first and He is the last. Our Lord Christ Jesus is the origin and source of all things and He was before all things (Col. 1:15-18).

Colossians 1:15-18

"Who is the image of the invisible God, the firstborn of every creature: For by him were all things created, that are in heaven, and that are in earth, visible and invisible, whether they be thrones, or dominions, or principalities, or powers: all things were created by him, and for him: And he is before all things, and by him all things consist. And he is the head of the body, the church: who is the beginning, the firstborn from the dead; that in all things he might have the preeminence."

Revelation 1:17

"And when I saw him, I fell at his feet as dead. And he laid his right hand upon me, saying unto me, Fear not; I am the first and the last."

Revelation 21:6

"And he said unto me, It is done. I am Alpha and Omega, the beginning and the end. I will give unto him that is athirst of the fountain of the water of life freely."

Isaiah 43:10-11

"Ye are my witnesses, saith the Lord, and my servant whom I have chosen: that ye may know

and believe me, and understand that I am he: before me there was no God formed, neither shall there be after me. I, even I, am the Lord; and beside me there is no Savior."

<u>Isaiah 48:12</u>

"Hearken unto me, O Jacob and Israel, my called; I am he; I am the first, I also am the last."

REVIEW

What does the title "Son" teach us?

The title "Son" reveals to us our Lord Jesus Christ's eternal existence. He existed in eternity past and was sent into the world to redeem His people from their sins.

What must sinners do in order to be saved from their sins?

They must receive the Son by faith as their Lord and Savior. Whoever believes in the Lord Jesus Christ will not perish, but will have everlasting life.

In the last days, how has God chosen to speak to His people?

God has spoken to His people by His Son, the Lord Jesus Christ, who is both Creator and Heir of all things.

What does the title "Son of man" teach us about our Lord Jesus Christ?

This title is a messianic title for our Lord Jesus Christ. It is the title by which He described Himself. He is fully God and fully man.

Where is the Son of man and what is His role at this time?

The Son of man is seated on the right hand of the power of God. He makes continual intercession for the people of God.

How will the Son of man return to the earth?

He will come in the clouds of heaven and all the holy angels with him, and then He will sit upon the throne of His glory.

What does the title "Lamb of God" reveal about our Lord Jesus Christ?

This title reveals that the Lord Jesus Christ was the One sent by God to serve as the perfect sinless sacrificial lamb for the sin of the world.

B. Divine Attributes of Christ Jesus

1. Omnipotence

This means that He is all powerful. He has power over death, over nature, over demons and over heaven and earth. He is God Almighty. As we pray to our Lord Christ Jesus, we should have this confidence that He has all authority.

Therefore, we should praise Him and trust that He is Lord of our circumstances. Our Lord Jesus is King of kings. He reigns on high.

    a. His Power over Heaven and Earth

Matthew 28:18

"And Jesus came and spake unto them, saying, All power is given unto me in heaven and in earth."

John 11:25-26

"Jesus said unto her, I am the resurrection, and the life: he that believeth in me, though he were dead, yet shall he live: And whosoever liveth and believeth in me shall never die. Believest thou this?"

Revelation 1:18

"I am he that liveth, and was dead; and, behold, I am alive for evermore, Amen; and have the keys of hell and of death."

    b. His Power over Nature

Colossians 1:16-17

"For by him were all things created, that are in heaven, and that are in earth, visible and invisible, whether they be thrones, or dominions, or principalities, or powers: all things were created by him, and for him: And he

is before all things, and by him all things consist."

Matthew 8:26

"And he saith unto them, Why are ye fearful, O ye of little faith? Then he arose, and rebuked the winds and the sea; and there was a great calm."

Matthew 14:25-27

"And in the fourth watch of the night Jesus went unto them, walking on the sea. And when the disciples saw him walking on the sea, they were troubled, saying, It is a spirit; and they cried out for fear. But straightway Jesus spake unto them, saying, Be of good cheer; it is I; be not afraid."

c. His Power over Demons

Matthew 8:28-32

"And when he was come to the other side into the country of the Gergesenes, there met him two possessed with devils, coming out of the tombs, exceeding fierce, so that no man might pass by that way. And, behold, they cried out, saying, What have we to do with thee, Jesus, thou Son of God? art thou come hither to torment us before the time? And there was a good way off from them an herd of many swine feeding. So the devils besought him, saying, If thou cast us out, suffer us to go away into the herd of swine. And he said unto them, Go. And when they were come out, they went into the herd of swine: and, behold, the whole herd of swine ran violently down a steep place into the sea, and perished in the waters."

Luke 4:35-36

"And Jesus rebuked him, saying, Hold thy peace, and come out of him. And when the devil had thrown him in the midst, he came out of him, and hurt him not. And they were all amazed, and spake among themselves, saying, What a word is this! for with authority and power he commandeth the unclean spirits, and they come out."

2. Omniscience

Omniscience means that Jesus is all knowing. Before the earth was created, He knew the destiny of all men. He knows the future and is working out His purpose for our lives. Our Lord Christ Jesus knows all our needs. Before we can cry out to Him in prayer, He knows and is ready to answer. What a comfort of assurance in trusting in our Lord who is omniscient.

John 21:17

"He saith unto him the third time, Simon, son of Jonah, lovest thou me? Peter was grieved because he said unto him the third time, Lovest thou me? And he said unto him, Lord, thou knowest all things; thou knowest that I love thee. Jesus saith unto him, Feed my sheep."

Matthew 9:4

"But Jesus, knowing their thoughts, said, Why do you think evil in your hearts?"

Mark 12:15

"Shall we give, or shall we not give? But he, knowing their hypocrisy, said unto them, Why tempt ye me? bring me a penny, that I may see it."

Luke 5:22

"But when Jesus perceived their thoughts, he answering said unto them, What reason ye in your hearts?"

Luke 6:8

"But he knew their thoughts, and said to the man which had the withered hand, Rise up, and stand forth in the midst. And he arose and stood forth."

Luke 11:17

"But he, knowing their thoughts, said unto them, Every kingdom divided against itself is brought to desolation; and a house divided against a house falleth."

Luke 12:7

"But even the very hairs of your head are all numbered. Fear not therefore: ye are of more value than many sparrows."

John 1:48

"Nathanael saith unto him, Whence knowest thou me? Jesus answered and said unto him, Before that Philip called thee, when thou wast under the fig tree, I saw thee."

John 2:25

"And needed not that any should testify of man: for he knew what was in man."

Psalm 139:2-4

"Thou knowest my downsitting and mine uprising, thou understandest my thought afar off. Thou compassest my path and my lying down, and art acquainted with all my ways. For there is not a word in my tongue, but, lo, O Lord, thou knowest it altogether."

3. Omnipresence

This means that our Lord Jesus Christ is everywhere present. He promised us that He will be with us always. We should have a sense of peace and lasting joy knowing that our Savior is always with us. Whatever trials may come our way, He is there to strengthen us.

Matthew 28:20

"Teaching them to observe all things whatsoever I have commanded you: and, lo, I am with you alway, even unto the end of the world. Amen."

Hebrews 13:5b

"...for he hath said, I will never leave thee, nor forsake thee."

Psalm 46:1

"God is our refuge and strength, a very present help in trouble."

4. Immutability

This means that He never changes. He is the same yesterday and today, and forever.

Hebrews 13:8

"Jesus Christ the same yesterday, and today, and for ever."

Hebrews 7:23-25

"And they truly were many priests, because they were not suffered to continue by reason of death: But this man, because he continueth ever, hath an unchangeable priesthood. Wherefore he is able also to save them to the

uttermost that come unto God by him, seeing he ever liveth to make intercession for them."

<u>Malachi 3:6a</u>

"For I am the LORD, I change not..."

5. Holiness

This means that there is no sin in Him. It was necessary that our holy, righteous God came and died for our sin. The name Christ Jesus means Anointed Savior. The word "anointed" means holy. Therefore, our Lord is the holy Savior.

<u>1 John 3:5</u>

"And ye know that he was manifested to take away our sins; and in him is no sin."

<u>2 Corinthians 5:21</u>

"For he hath made him to be sin for us, who knew no sin; that we might be made the righteousness of God in him."

<u>Hebrews 4:15</u>

"For we have not an high priest which cannot be touched with the feeling of our infirmities; but was in all points tempted like as we are, yet without sin."

1 Peter 1:19

"But with the precious blood of Christ, as of a lamb without blemish and without spot."

REVIEW

What does omnipotence tell us about Jesus' deity or divine nature?

It shows that He is God.

What is the meaning of the word omniscience?

It means all knowing.

What is the meaning of the word omnipresent?

It means that He is ever-present.

What is Jesus presently doing?

He is our High Priest. This means that He is always praying for us.

What is the meaning of the word immutable?

It means never changing.

C. The Incarnation of Christ Jesus

The word "incarnation" means "in the flesh." The mystery of the incarnation is that God came in the person of Christ Jesus in the flesh. Jesus' birth was not like others.

Mary, His earthly mother, was a virgin at His conception. She was engaged to Joseph. This conception was a result of the supernatural work of the Holy Spirit.

Luke 1:31

"And, behold, thou shalt conceive in thy womb, and bring forth a son, and shalt call his name Jesus."

Luke 1:34-35

"Then said Mary unto the angel, How shall this be, seeing I know not a man? And the angel answered and said unto her, The Holy Ghost shall come upon thee, and the power of the Highest shall overshadow thee: therefore also that holy thing which shall be born of thee shall be called the Son of God."

REVIEW

What is the meaning of the word "Incarnation"?

It means "in the flesh."

How did the conception of the Christ Child come about?

The Holy Spirit overshadowed Mary and performed a miracle in her womb which gave birth to the Christ Child.

1. Reasons for the Incarnation

    John 1:18

    "No man hath seen God at any time; the only begotten Son, which is in the bosom of the Father, he hath declared him."

    Why was it necessary for God Almighty to come in the form of flesh? Jesus came to reveal God to men.

    a. Jesus came to be an example for Christian living.

        1 Peter 2:21

        "For even hereunto were ye called: because Christ also suffered for us, leaving us an example, that ye should follow his steps."

    b. Jesus came to die for our sin.

        1 Corinthians 15:3

        "For I delivered unto you first of all that which I also received, how that Christ died for our sins according to the scriptures."

    c. Jesus came to destroy the works of the devil.

        1 John 3:8

        "He that committeth sin is of the devil; for the devil sinneth from the beginning. For this purpose the Son of God was manifested, that he might destroy the works of the devil."

Satan has already been defeated. As God's children, we are victorious in Him. Satan does not have victory over us. Certainly we are in a spiritual warfare. Praise be to God our Lord that He has destroyed the works of the devil.

    d. Jesus came in order to become our heavenly High Priest.

Hebrews 4:14-15

"Seeing then that we have a great high priest, that is passed into the heavens, Jesus the Son of God, let us hold fast our profession. For we have not an high priest which cannot be touched with the feeling of our infirmities; but was in all points tempted like as we are, yet without sin."

The fact that our Lord Christ Jesus is our eternal High Priest interceding on our behalf assures us of victory over Satan. Also, we have the comfort in knowing that our High Priest understands our hurt and pain. He invites us to come boldly to His throne of grace.

    e. Jesus came to fulfill the Davidic Covenant

Luke 1:31-33

"And, behold, thou shalt conceive in thy womb, and bring forth a Son, and shalt call his name JESUS. He shall be great, and shall be called the Son of the Highest: and the Lord God shall give unto him the throne of his father David: And he shall reign over the house of Jacob

for ever; and of his kingdom there shall be no end."

<u>2 Samuel 7:11b-13</u>

"Also the Lord telleth thee that he will make thee an house. And when thy days be fulfilled, and thou shalt sleep with thy fathers, I will set up thy seed after thee, which shall proceed out of thy bowels, and I will establish his kingdom. He shall build an house for my name, and I will establish the throne of his kingdom for ever."

2. The Humanity of Christ

Our Lord Christ Jesus is fully man yet fully God. He came in the form of flesh in order to die for our sins. The fact that He is fully God yet fully man is a mystery. We may not fully understand, however, He will help us to grow to experience Him as our Lord.

<u>1 Timothy 3:16</u>

"And without controversy great is the mystery of godliness: God was manifest in the flesh, justified in the Spirit, seen of angels, preached unto the Gentiles, believed on in the world, received up into glory."

<u>John 1:14</u>

"And the Word was made flesh, and dwelt among us, (and we beheld his glory, the glory

as of the only begotten of the Father), full of grace and truth."

Romans 1:3-4

"Concerning his Son Jesus Christ our Lord, which was made of the seed of David according to the flesh; And declared to be the Son of God with power, according to the spirit of holiness, by the resurrection from the dead."

a. Jesus had a human body. He was born of a woman. His earthly mother was Mary.

Galatians 4:4

"But when the fullness of the time was come, God sent forth his Son, made of a woman, made under the law."

b. Jesus had a human soul and spirit.

Matthew 26:38

"Then saith he unto them, My soul is exceeding sorrowful, even unto death: tarry ye here, and watch with me."

Luke 23:46

"And when Jesus had cried with a loud voice, he said, Father, into thy hands I commend my spirit: and having said thus, he gave up the ghost."

c. Jesus was subject to the limitations of humanity.

   (1) He hungered.

   Matthew 4:2

   "And when he had fasted forty days and forty nights, he was afterward an hungered."

   (2) He was thirsty.

   John 19:28

   "After this, Jesus knowing that all things were now accomplished, that the Scripture might be fulfilled, saith, I thirst."

   (3) He grew weary.

   John 4:6

   "Now Jacob's well was there. Jesus therefore, being wearied with his journey, sat thus on the well: and it was about the sixth hour."

   (4) He was tempted.

   Hebrews 4:15

   "For we have not an high priest which cannot be touched with the feeling of our infirmities; but was in all points tempted like as we are, yet without sin."

(5) He wept.

John 11:35

"Jesus wept."

Luke 19:41

"And when he was come near, he beheld the city, and wept over it."

d. Jesus had human names.

(1) He was called "Son of man."

Luke 19:10

"For the Son of man is come to seek and to save that which was lost."

(2) His earthly name is Jesus.

Matthew 1:21

"And she shall bring forth a son, and thou shalt call his name Jesus: for he shall save his people from their sins."

(3) He was called "Son of David."

Mark 10:47

"And when he heard that it was Jesus of Nazareth, he began to cry out, and say,

Jesus, thou Son of David, have mercy on me."

(4) He was called man.

1 Corinthians 15:47

"The first man is of the earth, earthy: the second man is the Lord from heaven."

1 Timothy 2:5

"For there is one God, and one mediator between God and men, the man Christ Jesus."

Acts 2:22

"Ye men of Israel, hear these words; Jesus of Nazareth, a man approved of God among you by miracles and wonders and signs, which God did by him in the midst of you, as ye yourselves also know."

(5) He experienced physical death.

Luke 23:46

"And when Jesus had cried with a loud voice, he said, Father, into thy hands I commend my spirit: and having said thus, he gave up the ghost."

1 Corinthians 15:3

"For I delivered unto you first of all that which I also received, how that Christ died for our sins according to the scriptures."

1 Peter 1:3

"Blessed be the God and Father of our Lord Jesus Christ, which according to his abundant mercy hath begotten us again unto a lively hope by the resurrection of Jesus Christ from the dead."

Chapter 3

THE DOCTRINE OF THE HOLY SPIRIT

A. The Nature and Work of the Holy Spirit

The Holy Spirit is the Spirit of God. The Greek word for the Holy Spirit means wind or breath. The Holy Spirit is the breath of God. Only the Bible can accurately explain and instruct on God's Holy Spirit. Only Christians can experience the Holy Spirit because He was given to the church by Jesus Christ.

The primary work of the Holy Spirit is to glorify Christ Jesus. The Spirit does not speak about Himself; He seeks to declare Christ Jesus (John 16:13-15).

<u>John 16:13-15</u>

"Howbeit when he, the Spirit of truth, is come, he will guide you into all truth: for he shall not speak of himself; but whatsoever he shall hear, that shall he speak: and he will show you things to come. He shall glorify me: for he shall receive of mine, and shall show it unto you. All things

that the Father hath are mine: therefore said I, that he shall take of mine, and shall show it unto you."

Another purpose of the Holy Spirit is to seal believers, that is, to spiritually mark believers as possessions of God and possessors of eternal life (Eph.1:13). When someone accepts Christ Jesus as their Lord and Savior, that person experiences what the Bible calls "the baptism of the Holy Spirit" (1 Cor. 12:13). This is a work of the Holy Spirit by which He begins to transform the believer into the image of Jesus Christ. The believer, then, begins to allow the Holy Spirit to control his spirit. However, it is possible that, by an act of their will, believers can hinder the Holy Spirit from leading them.

Ephesians 1:13

"In whom ye also trusted, after that ye heard the word of truth, the Gospel of your salvation: in whom also after that ye believed, ye were sealed with that Holy Spirit of promise."

1 Corinthians 12:13

"For by one Spirit are we all baptized into one body, whether we be Jews or Gentiles, whether we be bond or free; and have been all made to drink into one Spirit."

As we study the doctrine or teaching of the Holy Spirit, let us keep two very important factors in mind. First, as Christians, the Holy Spirit is present in us controlling and empowering our lives. And secondly, the Holy Spirit always seeks to glorify Christ, not Himself.

REVIEW

What is the main function of the Holy Spirit?

The main purpose of the Holy Spirit is to glorify our Lord Christ Jesus.

What is the meaning of the Greek word for the Holy Spirit?

It means breath or wind.

B. The Personality of the Holy Spirit

Scripture clearly shows that the Holy Spirit is a person, and should not be referred to as "it." He possesses all of the attributes of personality.

1. The Holy Spirit possesses intelligence.

   <u>1 Corinthians 2:11</u>

   "For what man knoweth the things of a man, save the spirit of man which is in him? even so the things of God knoweth no man, but the Spirit of God."

2. The Holy Spirit possesses a will.

   <u>1 Corinthians 12:11</u>

   "But all these worketh that one and the selfsame Spirit, dividing to every man severally as he will."

3. The Holy Spirit possesses power.

   Luke 4:14

   "And Jesus returned in the power of the Spirit into Galilee: and there went out a fame of him through all the region round about."

   Luke 24:49

   "And, behold, I send the promise of my Father upon you: but tarry ye in the city of Jerusalem, until ye be endued with power from on high."

   Acts 1:8

   "But ye shall receive power, after that the Holy Ghost is come upon you: and ye shall be witnesses unto me both in Jerusalem, and in all Judea, and in Samaria, and unto the uttermost part of the earth."

   Romans 15:18-19

   "For I will not dare to speak of any of those things which Christ hath not wrought by me, to make the Gentiles obedient, by word and deed, Through mighty signs and wonders, by the power of the Spirit of God; so that from Jerusalem, and round about unto Illyricum, I have fully preached the Gospel of Christ."

4. The Holy Spirit possesses knowledge.

   1 Corinthians 2:10-12

   "But God hath revealed them unto us by his Spirit: for the Spirit searcheth all things, yea, the deep things of God. For what man knoweth the things of a man, save the spirit of man which is in him? Even so the things of God knoweth no man, but the Spirit of God. Now we have received, not the spirit of the world, but the spirit which is of God; that we might know the things that are freely given to us of God."

5. The Holy Spirit possesses love.

   Romans 15:30

   "Now I beseech you, brethren, for the Lord Jesus Christ's sake, and for the love of the Spirit, that ye strive together with me in your prayers to God for me."

   Romans 5:5

   "And hope maketh not ashamed; because the love of God is shed abroad in our hearts by the Holy Ghost which is given unto us."

REVIEW

What are the Holy Spirit's traits of personality?

The traits of personality which the Holy Spirit demonstrates are:

- Intelligence
- Will
- Power
- Knowledge
- Love

C. The Activity of the Holy Spirit

The Holy Spirit is a person who is capable of performing acts as He desires. In Scripture, personal pronouns used pertaining to the Holy Spirit are always masculine in gender. At this point we shall examine the works of the Holy Spirit.

1. The Holy Spirit speaks.

Mark 13:11

> "But when they shall lead you, and deliver you up, take no thought beforehand what ye shall speak, neither do ye premeditate: but whatsoever shall be given you in that hour, that speak ye: for it is not ye that speak, but the Holy Ghost."

Acts 8:29

"Then the Spirit said unto Philip, Go near, and join thyself to this chariot."

Acts 10:19-20

"While Peter thought on the vision, the Spirit said unto him, Behold, three men seek thee. Arise therefore, and get thee down, and go with them, doubting nothing: for I have sent them."

Acts 13:2

"As they ministered to the Lord, and fasted, the Holy Ghost said, Separate me Barnabas and Saul for the work whereunto I have called them."

1 Timothy 4:1

"Now the Spirit speaketh expressly, that in the latter times some shall depart from the faith, giving heed to seducing spirits, and doctrines of devils."

2. The Holy Spirit intercedes.

Romans 8:26

"Likewise the Spirit also helpeth our infirmities: for we know not what we should pray for as we ought: but the Spirit itself maketh inter-

cession for us with groanings which cannot be uttered."

3. The Holy Spirit testifies.

John 15:26

"But when the Comforter is come, whom I will send unto you from the Father, even the Spirit of truth, which proceedeth from the Father, he shall testify of me."

4. The Holy Spirit commands.

Acts 8:29

"Then the Spirit said unto Philip, Go near, and join thyself to this chariot."

Acts 10:19-20

"While Peter thought on the vision, the Spirit said unto him, Behold, three men seek thee. Arise therefore, and get thee down, and go with them, doubting nothing: for I have sent them."

Acts 11:12

"And the Spirit bade me go with them, nothing doubting. Moreover these six brethren accompanied me, and we entered into the man's house."

5. The Holy Spirit restrains.

    Acts 16:6-7

    "Now when they had gone throughout Phrygia and the region of Galatia, and were forbidden of the Holy Ghost to preach the word in Asia, After they were come to Mysia, they assayed to go into Bithynia: but the Spirit suffered them not."

6. The Holy Spirit guides.

    John 16:13a

    "Howbeit when he, the Spirit of truth, is come, he will guide you into all truth..."

    Luke 2:27

    "And he came by the Spirit into the temple: and when the parents brought in the child Jesus, to do for him after the custom of the law,"

    Luke 4:1

    "And Jesus being full of the Holy Ghost returned from Jordan, and was led by the Spirit into the wilderness."

7. The Holy Spirit teaches.

   John 14:26

   "But the Comforter, which is the Holy Ghost, whom the Father will send in my name, he shall teach you all things, and bring all things to your remembrance, whatsoever I have said unto you."

   1 Corinthians 2:13

   "Which things also we speak, not in the words which man's wisdom teacheth, but which the Holy Ghost teacheth; comparing spiritual things with spiritual."

   Luke 12:11-12

   "And when they bring you unto the synagogues, and unto magistrates, and powers, take ye no thought how or what thing ye shall answer, or what ye shall say: For the Holy Ghost shall teach you in the same hour what ye ought to say."

8. The Holy Spirit commissions.

   Acts 13:4

   "So they, being sent forth by the Holy Ghost, departed unto Seleucia; and from thence they sailed to Cyprus."

9. The Holy Spirit reveals.

Luke 2:25-26

"And, behold, there was a man in Jerusalem, whose name was Simeon; and the same man was just and devout, waiting for the consolation of Israel: and the Holy Ghost was upon him. And it was revealed unto him by the Holy Ghost, that he should not see death, before he had seen the Lord's Christ."

Acts 11:28

"And there stood up one of them named Agabus, and signified by the Spirit that there should be great dearth throughout all the world: which came to pass in the days of Claudius Caesar."

Ephesians 3:3-6

"How that by revelation he made known unto me the mystery; (as I wrote afore in few words, Whereby, when ye read, ye may understand my knowledge in the mystery of Christ) Which in other ages was not made known unto the sons of men, as it is now revealed unto his holy apostles and prophets by the Spirit; That the Gentiles should be fellow heirs, and of the same body, and partakers of his promise in Christ by the Gospel."

REVIEW

What are the personal acts of the Holy Spirit?

The personal acts of the Holy Spirit are:

- He speaks
- He intercedes
- He testifies
- He commands
- He restrains
- He guides
- He teaches
- He commissions
  He reveals

D. Resisting the Holy Spirit

The Holy Spirit is fully God and co-equal with the Father and the Son. However, He does not force persons to submit to Him. Each believer has to acknowledge the Lordship of the Spirit in His life by an act of his or her will. God gives us a free will to accept Jesus as our Savior. Similarly, we have the free will to yield to the Holy Spirit or to reject His influence.

Let us consider what some of the acts are which can be committed against the Holy Spirit.

1. The Holy Spirit may be grieved.

   Ephesians 4:30

   "And grieve not the Holy Spirit of God, whereby ye are sealed unto the day of redemption."

A believer who sins is said to grieve the Holy Spirit. The word "grieve" means "to cause pain." The Spirit is pained by sin. The believer who is in sin should repent. This means that that person should confess the wrongdoing before God and ask God's forgiveness. After confession, the believer should obey God's Word and do what is pleasing to Him (1 John 1:9).

1 John 1:9

"If we confess our sins, he is faithful and just to forgive us our sins, and to cleanse us from all unrighteousness."

2. The Holy Spirit may be tested.

Acts 5:9

"Then Peter said unto her, How is it that ye have agreed together to tempt the Spirit of the Lord? behold, the feet of them which have buried thy husband are at the door, and shall carry thee out."

To test means to see how far someone can go in taking for granted God's goodness. The individual who tests the Spirit is one who is seeking his own selfish desires. God wants us to seek His will for our life. Our Lord Christ Jesus must not only be our Savior, but also Lord of our lives.

3. The Holy Spirit may be resisted.

Acts 7:51

"Ye stiffnecked and uncircumcised in heart and ears, ye do always resist the Holy Ghost: as your fathers did, so do ye."

To resist the Holy Spirit is to harden our hearts to the leading of the Holy Spirit.

4. The Holy Spirit may be blasphemed.

Mark 3:29-30

"But he that shall blaspheme against the Holy Ghost hath never forgiveness, but is in danger of eternal damnation: Because they said, He hath an unclean spirit."

Mark 3:22 states, "And the scribes which came down from Jerusalem said, He hath Beelzebub, and by the prince of the devils casteth he out devils." In this verse, the Holy Spirit had been blasphemed because the Pharisees accused Jesus of working His miracles by the power of Satan. In truth, it was the Holy Spirit who empowered Jesus to do His mighty works. A person who rejects the leading of the Holy Spirit rejects the only means by which he can repent of sin and receive saving faith. That is why for that person, there can be no forgiveness.

REVIEW

What are four acts which someone may commit against the Holy Spirit?

The Holy Spirit may be:

- Grieved
- Tested
- Resisted
- Blasphemed

E. The Holy Spirit and Christ Jesus

The Holy Spirit is God and is the third person of the Godhead. Even though He is co-equal with the Father and the Son, His primary work is to glorify Christ Jesus. It is the Holy Spirit who draws a person to Christ and empowers him or her for godly works. The Holy Spirit was especially active during Christ's earthly ministry.

1. He caused Christ's conception in Mary's womb.

    Luke 1:34-35

    "Then said Mary unto the angel, How shall this be, seeing I know not a man? And the angel answered and said unto her, The Holy Ghost shall come upon thee, and the power of the Highest shall overshadow thee: therefore also that holy thing which shall be born of thee shall be called the Son of God."

2. He anointed Christ.

   Luke 4:18

   "The Spirit of the Lord is upon me, because he hath anointed me to preach the Gospel to the poor; he hath sent me to heal the brokenhearted, to preach deliverance to the captives, and recovering of sight to the blind, to set at liberty them that are bruised."

3. He led Christ.

   Luke 4:1

   "And Jesus being full of the Holy Ghost returned from Jordan, and was led by the Spirit into the wilderness."

4. He empowered Christ.

   Matthew 12:28

   "But if I cast out devils by the Spirit of God, then the kingdom of God is come unto you."

   Luke 4:14

   "And Jesus returned in the power of the Spirit into Galilee: and there went out a fame of him through all the region round about."

5. He brought about the resurrection of Christ.

   1 Peter 3:18

   "For Christ also hath once suffered for sins, the just for the unjust, that he might bring us to God, being put to death in the flesh, but quickened by the Spirit."

   Romans 8:11

   "But if the Spirit of him that raised up Jesus from the dead dwell in you, he that raised up Christ from the dead shall also quicken your mortal bodies by his Spirit that dwelleth in you."

6. He glorifies Christ.

   John 16:14

   "He shall glorify me: for he shall receive of mine, and shall show it unto you."

   John 15:26

   "But when the Comforter is come, whom I will send unto you from the Father, even the Spirit of truth, which proceedeth from the Father, he shall testify of me."

The main work of the Holy Spirit is to bring glory or worship to Christ Jesus. As the believer grows spiritually this work of the Holy Spirit will become more obvious through that Christian's life. Whatever we do, whether in words or deeds, we should do all things to glorify our Lord.

Romans 15:7

"Wherefore receive ye one another, as Christ also received us to the glory of God."

1 Corinthians 10:31

"Whether therefore ye eat, or drink, or whatsoever ye do, do all to the glory of God."

2 Corinthians 4:15

"For all things are for your sakes, that the abundant grace might through the thanksgiving of many redound to the glory of God."

Philippians 2:11

"And that every tongue should confess that Jesus Christ is Lord, to the glory of God the Father."

1 Corinthians 6:19-20

"What? know ye not that your body is the temple of the Holy Ghost which is in you, which ye have of God, and ye are not your own? For ye are bought with a price: therefore glorify God in your body, and in your spirit, which are God's."

F. The Holy Spirit's Relationship with Mankind

The Word of God tells us that after we accept Christ Jesus as our Savior we are sealed with the Holy Spirit. Ephesians 1:13 states, "In whom ye also trusted, after that ye heard the word of truth, the Gospel of your salvation: in whom also after that ye believed, ye were sealed with that Holy Spirit of promise." This sealing of the Holy Spirit indicates possession and security. This is the believer's guarantee that he is saved and will always be saved for all eternity. After this sealing, the Holy Spirit now has a special relationship with the believer. Let us consider this relationship.

1. The Convicting Work of the Holy Spirit

John 16:8

"And when he is come, he will reprove the world of sin, and of righteousness, and of judgment."

The Holy Spirit causes the unbeliever to come into a right relationship with God. The Spirit does this work by convicting the heart of men. The word convict means to place the truth of the Gospel message in the heart of the unsaved. The individual has to make a choice to accept or reject the Gospel message.

2. The Regenerating Work of the Holy Spirit

Titus 3:4-5

"But after that the kindness and love of God our Savior toward man appeared, Not by

> *works of righteousness which we have done, but according to his mercy he saved us, by the washing of regeneration, and renewing of the Holy Ghost."*

Another work of the Holy Spirit in men is regeneration. Regeneration is an act of God in the heart of the unsaved by which He creates in a person a new nature that is holy and desirous of fellowship with God. How then does regeneration work? First, the Holy Spirit uses the Word of God to convict the unbeliever. The individual then responds by faith in the Gospel of Jesus Christ. The Holy Spirit then regenerates the person and he is born again.

3. The Indwelling of the Holy Spirit

<u>1 Corinthians 6:19</u>

> *"What? know ye not that your body is the temple of the Holy Ghost which is in you, which ye have of God, and ye are not your own?"*

<u>1 Corinthians 3:16</u>

> *"Know ye not that ye are the temple of God, and that the Spirit of God dwelleth in you?"*

The Holy Spirit indwells the believer, that is, He becomes present in the being of the believer. The very body of the believer becomes the temple of the Holy Spirit. Knowing that the Holy Spirit dwells in us, we should obey God's Word and keep ourselves holy. We should live our lives in a manner that is pleasing to God, and always seek to glorify Christ Jesus our Lord.

4. The Baptizing Work of the Holy Spirit

The baptism of the Holy Spirit is experienced by every believer. It takes place at the time of salvation. This work of the Spirit takes place only once. This baptism did not take place before Pentecost, that is, before the Holy Spirit began the work as described in Acts 2. The baptism of the Holy Spirit puts the believer into the body of Christ which is the church. This baptism is different from water baptism. Water baptism is a public rite in which a believer professes his faith in Jesus Christ and identifies himself with Christ's death, burial and resurrection. The baptism of the Holy Spirit is a spiritual work and is a past event at the time of water baptism.

    a. Baptism began in the early Church.

Acts 1:5

"*For John truly baptized with water; but ye shall be baptized with the Holy Ghost not many days hence.*"

    b. Baptism involves all believers.

1 Corinthians 12:13

"*For by one Spirit are we all baptized into one body, whether we be Jews or Gentiles, whether we be bond or free; and have been all made to drink into one Spirit.*"

c. Baptism happens only once.

1 Corinthians 12:13

"For by one Spirit are we all baptized into one body, whether we be Jews or Gentiles, whether we be bond or free; and have been all made to drink into one Spirit."

Ephesians 4:4-5

"There is one body, and one Spirit, even as ye are called in one hope of your calling; One Lord, one faith, one baptism."

The verb "baptized" in this verse is used in what is called the aorist tense. This means that the action is a one-time event, that is, it occurred once with an on-going effect. Thus, we are baptized into the body of Christ which is the church, and this happened only once.

5. The Gifts of the Holy Spirit

1 Corinthians 12:4-7

"Now there are diversities of gifts, but the same Spirit. And there are differences of administrations, but the same Lord. And there are diversities of operations, but it is the same God which worketh all in all. But the manifestation of the Spirit is given to every man to profit withal."

1 Corinthians 12:11

"But all these worketh that one and the selfsame Spirit, dividing to every man severally as he will."

The Holy Spirit empowers believers with spiritual gifts. A spiritual gift is a God-given ability for service.

Romans 12:6-8

"Having then gifts differing according to the grace that is given to us, whether prophecy, let us prophesy according to the proportion of faith; or ministry, let us wait on our ministering: or he that teacheth, on teaching; or he that exhorteth, on exhortation: he that giveth, let him do it with simplicity; he that ruleth, with diligence; he that showeth mercy, with cheerfulness."

Ephesians 4:11

"And he gave some, apostles; and some, prophets; and some, evangelists; and some, pastors and teachers."

1 Peter 4:10

"As every man hath received the gift, even so minister the same one to another, as good stewards of the manifold grace of God."

REVIEW

Who is the Holy Spirit?

The Holy Spirit is God and co-equal with God the Father and God the Son. Together these three make up the Godhead.

What is the relationship between the Spirit and the Lord Christ Jesus?

The Holy Spirit's primary purpose is to glorify Christ Jesus.

What part did the Holy Spirit play in the resurrection?

The Holy Spirit raised Jesus from the dead.

How does the Holy Spirit draw someone to a right relationship with Christ?

The Spirit leads believers to proclaim the Gospel message. He then uses the Word of God to convict the unbeliever of His sinful condition and His need for a Savior.

When does the baptism of the Holy Spirit take place?

It occurs at the time of salvation.

When did the first baptism of the Holy Spirit take place?

It took place at Pentecost as the disciples and others were praying in the upper room.

How often do we need to be baptized?

The baptism of the Holy Spirit takes place only once in the believer's life. At the very moment of salvation, the believer experiences the baptism of the Holy Spirit.

What are spiritual gifts?

Spiritual gifts are God-given abilities for service.

What are three examples of spiritual gifts?

Three examples of spiritual gifts are apostles, prophets, and evangelists (Eph. 4:11).

G. The Filling of the Holy Spirit

God commands believers to be filled with the Spirit. The Holy Spirit enables us to live holy and righteously. This is because our God is holy and righteous. 1 Peter 1:16 reads in part, ". . . Be holy, for I am holy." When we sin, we must confess our sins so that we may be cleansed from all unrighteousness. We are commanded to continually yield to the Holy Spirit. By faith, we have to accept the control of the Holy Spirit and obey God's Word. We must accept the Lordship of Christ Jesus over us. In order to experience the filling of the Holy Spirit, we have to be in total dependence upon the Holy Spirit. This acceptance of our dependency must begin with the acknowledgement of God's grace in our lives. We are saved and kept by His grace. It is God's grace that we have been chosen by Him to serve Him. His grace carries us through the trials and stresses of life. This attitude of humility allows us to be receptive to the leading of the Holy Spirit.

1. The Holy Spirit and the Believer

   Romans 8:9b

   "...Now if any man have not the Spirit of Christ, he is none of his."

The filling of the Spirit is different from the baptism of the Spirit. Baptism takes place at the point of salvation. To be filled by the Spirit means to be controlled by the Spirit. The filling may also take place at the point of salvation or may take place later on. A believer may experience many different times of the filling of the Spirit. Therefore, even though someone may be sealed or baptized in the Spirit, that person may not have experienced the filling. Certainly all believers have the Spirit, but not everyone is filled with the Spirit. It is possible that a believer can grieve the Holy Spirit and hinder Him from working through his life. By yielding to the Spirit, the believer presents himself as a living sacrifice to God.

   Romans 12:1

   "I beseech you therefore, brethren, by the mercies of God, that ye present your bodies a living sacrifice, holy, acceptable unto God, which is your reasonable service."

The term "reasonable service" means that yielding ourselves totally to God is the only right response of the believer to God's grace. As the believer yields to the Holy Spirit, he experiences the filling. The filling of the Spirit is that state in which the Holy Spirit works in and through a person unhindered. When we are filled with the Spirit, we experience Christ's purpose in our lives. The filling of the Spirit will produce the fruit of the Spirit in us. The fruit of the Spirit will actually change our character. Galatians 5:22-23 states, "But the fruit of the Spirit is love, joy, peace, longsuffering, gentleness, goodness, faith, Meekness, temperance..."

God's desire is that every believer lives continually in the state of being filled and controlled by His Holy Spirit.

2. Nature of Being Filled with the Spirit

    a. Being filled means being controlled by God's Spirit.

Ephesians 5:18

"And be not drunk with wine, wherein is excess; but be filled with the Spirit."

    b. The filling of the Spirit is repeated.

Acts 2:4

"And they were all filled with the Holy Ghost, and began to speak with other tongues, as the Spirit gave them utterance."

Acts 4:8

"Then Peter, filled with the Holy Ghost, said unto them, Ye rulers of the people, and elders of Israel."

Acts 4:31

"And when they had prayed, the place was shaken where they were assembled together;

and they were all filled with the Holy Ghost, and they spake the Word of God with boldness."

Acts 7:55-56

"But he, being full of the Holy Ghost, looked up steadfastly into heaven, and saw the glory of God, and Jesus standing on the right hand of God, And said, Behold, I see the heavens opened, and the Son of man standing on the right hand of God."

Acts 9:17

"And Ananias went his way, and entered into the house; and putting his hands on him said, Brother Saul, the Lord, even Jesus, that appeared unto thee in the way as thou camest, hath sent me, that thou mightest receive thy sight, and be filled with the Holy Ghost."

Acts 13:52

"And the disciples were filled with joy, and with the Holy Ghost."

c. Filling of the Spirit produces Christlikeness.

Galatians 2:20

"I am crucified with Christ: nevertheless I live; yet not I, but Christ liveth in me: and the life which I now live in the flesh I live by the faith of the Son of God, who loved me, and gave himself for me."

Galatians 5:22-23

"But the fruit of the Spirit is love, joy, peace, longsuffering, gentleness, goodness, faith, meekness, temperance: against such there is no law."

   d. Filling of the Spirit is a command.

Ephesians 5:18b

"...but be filled with the Spirit."

REVIEW

What four factors describe the nature of being filled with the Spirit?

The four factors that describe the nature of being filled with the Spirit are:

- Being filled means being controlled by God's Spirit.
- Filling of the Spirit is repeated.
- Filling of the Spirit produces Christlikeness.
- Filling of the Spirit is a command.

3. Requirement for Being Filled with the Spirit

It is necessary for believers to read the Bible. The Word of God gives us the requirements for being filled with the Spirit. What then are the scriptural requirements for being filled with the Spirit?

a. Filling requires a life cleansed from the practice of sin.

   Ephesians 4:30

   "And grieve not the Holy Spirit of God, whereby ye are sealed unto the day of redemption."

   1 John 1:7-9

   "But if we walk in the light, as he is in the light, we have fellowship one with another, and the blood of Jesus Christ his Son cleanseth us from all sin. If we say that we have no sin, we deceive ourselves, and the truth is not in us. If we confess our sins, he is faithful and just to forgive us our sins, and to cleanse us from all unrighteousness."

b. Filling requires a life yielded to the control of the Holy Spirit.

   Romans 12:1-2

   "I beseech you therefore, brethren, by the mercies of God, that ye present your bodies a living sacrifice, holy, acceptable unto God, which is your reasonable service. And be not conformed to this world: but be ye transformed by the renewing of your mind, that ye may prove what is that good, and acceptable, and perfect, will of God."

Romans 6:13

"Neither yield ye your members as instruments of unrighteousness unto sin: but yield yourselves unto God, as those that are alive from the dead, and your members as instruments of righteousness unto God."

c. Filling requires a life dependent on the Holy Spirit.

Ephesians 5:18

"And be not drunk with wine, wherein is excess; but be filled with the Spirit."

John 15:5

"I am the vine, ye are the branches: He that abideth in me, and I in him, the same bringeth forth much fruit: for without me ye can do nothing."

John 15:16

"Ye have not chosen me, but I have chosen you, and ordained you, that ye should go and bring forth fruit, and that your fruit should remain: that whatsoever ye shall ask of the Father in my name, he may give it you."

REVIEW

What are the conditions for being filled with the Spirit?

The conditions for being filled with the Spirit are:

- · a life free from sin
- · a life dependent on the Holy Spirit
- · a life yielded to the control of the Holy Spirit

H. The Deity of the Holy Spirit

The Holy Spirit of God is co-equal, co-eternal, and co-existent with the Father and the Son. He is one of three persons of the Trinity. Even though He is one with the Father and the Son, He is different in function. He seeks to glorify the Son and not Himself. The Father, the Son and the Holy Spirit are the same in substance. The word "substance" means an essential, native, fundamental, basic or characteristic part. This means that in the Trinity, all persons are equal in nature and characteristic. The Holy Spirit has all of the essential and moral attributes of God.

1. The Holy Spirit is omnipotent.

   Luke 1:35

   > *"And the angel answered and said unto her, The Holy Ghost shall come upon thee, and the power of the Highest shall overshadow thee: therefore also that holy thing which shall be born of thee shall be called the Son of God."*

2. The Holy Spirit is omniscient.

1 Corinthians 2:10-11

"But God hath revealed them unto us by his Spirit: for the Spirit searcheth all things, yea, the deep things of God. For what man knoweth the things of a man, save the spirit of man which is in him? even so the things of God knoweth no man, but the Spirit of God."

3. The Holy Spirit is omnipresent.

Psalm 139:7-10

"Whither shall I go from thy spirit? or whither shall I flee from thy presence? If I ascend up into heaven, thou art there: if I make my bed in hell, behold, thou art there. If I take the wings of the morning, and dwell in the uttermost parts of the sea; Even there shall thy hand lead me, and thy right hand shall hold me."

4. The Holy Spirit is eternal.

Hebrews 9:14

"How much more shall the blood of Christ, who through the eternal Spirit offered himself without spot to God, purge your conscience from dead works to serve the living God?"

5. The Holy Spirit performed uniquely divine works.

There are three works which are ascribed to God alone. These are creation, the imparting of life, and the authoring of Scripture.

a. The Holy Spirit participated in the creation.

Job 33:4

"The Spirit of God hath made me, and the breath of the Almighty hath given me life."

b. The Holy Spirit gives life.

John 6:63

"It is the Spirit that quickeneth; the flesh profiteth nothing: the words that I speak unto you, they are spirit, and they are life."

c. The Holy Spirit authored Scripture.

2 Peter 1:21

"For the prophecy came not in old time by the will of man: but holy men of God spake as they were moved by the Holy Ghost."

REVIEW

How do we know that the Holy Spirit is God?

We know that the Holy Spirit is God because He displays the essential attributes of God which are:

- Omnipotence
- Omniscience
- Omnipresence
- Eternalness

What works of the Holy Spirit prove that He is God?

The Holy Spirit has performed works that are uniquely divine:

- He created.
- He gave life.
- He authored Scripture.

Chapter 4

ECCLESIOLOGY

A. The Church

Ecclesiology is the study of the doctrine of the church. The word "church" means "a called-out company, or assembly." There are four different usages for the word church.

1. Church (a local assembly)

   <u>1 Thessalonians 1:1</u>

   "Paul, and Silvanus, and Timothy, unto the church of the Thessalonians which is in God the Father and in the Lord Jesus Christ: Grace be unto you, and peace, from God our Father, and the Lord Jesus Christ."

   <u>1 Corinthians 1:2</u>

   "Unto the church of God which is at Corinth, to them that are sanctified in Christ Jesus, called to be saints, with all that in every place

call upon the name of Jesus Christ our Lord, both theirs and ours."

2. Church (local assemblies)

   <u>Galatians 1:1-3</u>

   "Paul, an apostle, (not of men, neither by man, but by Jesus Christ, and God the Father, who raised him from the dead;) And all the brethren which are with me, unto the churches of Galatia: Grace be to you and peace from God the Father, and from our Lord Jesus Christ."

3. Church (the body of living believers)

   <u>Galatians 1:13</u>

   "For ye have heard of my conversation in time past in the Jews' religion, how that beyond measure I persecuted the church of God, and wasted it."

This refers to believers in a certain region, not believers worldwide, yet not believers in the local assembly.

4. Church (the complete body of Christ)

   <u>Ephesians 5:25</u>

   "Husbands, love your wives, even as Christ also loved the church, and gave himself for it."

The complete body of Christ refers to all believers worldwide, that is, all believers from Pentecost to the Rapture. This includes all who have and will accept Jesus as their personal Savior.

B. The Meaning of the Church

1. The church is a mystery.

   Ephesians 3:3-6

   "How that by revelation he made known unto me the mystery; (as I wrote afore in few words, Whereby, when ye read, ye may understand my knowledge in the mystery of Christ) Which in other ages was not made known unto the sons of men, as it is now revealed unto his holy apostles and prophets by the Spirit; That the Gentiles should be fellow heirs, and of the same body, and partakers of his promise in Christ by the Gospel."

   The word "mystery" in Scripture means a truth revealed for the first time. In the New Testament, the church was revealed for the first time to the Apostles. Part of this mystery is that the Gentiles may be saved through Christ Jesus.

2. The church is the body of which Christ Jesus is the Head.

   1 Corinthians 12:12-13

   "For as the body is one, and hath many members, and all the members of that one body, being many, are one body: so also is

> Christ. For by one Spirit are we all baptized into one body, whether we be Jews or Gentiles, whether we be bond or free; and have been all made to drink into one Spirit."

<u>*1 Corinthians 12:26-27*</u>

> "And whether one member suffer, all the members suffer with it; or one member be honored, all the members rejoice with it. Now ye are the body of Christ, and members in particular."

<u>*Colossians 1:18*</u>

> "And he (Christ Jesus) is the head of the body, the church: who is the beginning, the firstborn from the dead; that in all things he might have the preeminence."

The church is an organism which is composed of many members. This organism is called the body of Christ. The body belongs to Christ. Christ Jesus is Lord or Head of the body. In the Scriptures, the physical body is compared to the spiritual body. If one member of the body suffers, then all the other members suffer with it. If one member rejoices, then all other members rejoice with it. This unity and oneness of the body is possible because the believer is baptized into the body at salvation.

The purpose of the body is to reveal Christ to the world. The body has the great commission or calling by God to go to the ends of the earth and proclaim the Gospel message, that is, that Jesus Christ is Savior of the world. Salvation is only possible through faith in Christ's finished work on the cross. Salvation is a gift from God. No one can work for it.

Salvation must be received by belief that Jesus is Lord (Eph. 2:8-9).

> *Ephesians 2:8-9*
>
> *"For by grace are ye saved through faith; and that not of yourselves: it is the gift of God: Not of works, lest any man should boast."*
>
> *Matthew 28:19*
>
> *"Go ye therefore, and teach all nations, baptizing them in the name of the Father, and of the Son, and of the Holy Ghost."*
>
> *Acts 1:8*
>
> *"But ye shall receive power, after that the Holy Ghost is come upon you: and ye shall be witnesses unto me both in Jerusalem, and in all Judea, and in Samaria, and unto the uttermost part of the earth."*
>
> *Mark 16:15*
>
> *"And he said unto them, Go ye into all the world, and preach the Gospel to every creature."*

3. The church is a spiritual building or house.

> *Ephesians 2:19-20*
>
> *"Now therefore ye are no more strangers and foreigners, but fellow citizens with the*

> saints, and of the household of God; And are built upon the foundation of the apostles and prophets, Jesus Christ himself being the chief corner stone."

1 Peter 2:5

> "Ye also, as lively stones, are built up a spiritual house, an holy priesthood, to offer up spiritual sacrifices, acceptable to God by Jesus Christ."

Scripture describes the church as a spiritual building. This building is built on the foundation of the apostles and prophets. The chief cornerstone or main pillar of this building is our Lord Jesus Christ. This building has also been referred to as a household.

4. The church is the bride.

Ephesians 5:25

> "Husbands, love your wives, even as Christ also loved the church, and gave himself for it."

1 Corinthians 6:19-20

> "What? Know ye not that your body is the temple of the Holy Ghost which is in you, which ye have of God, and ye are not your own? For ye are bought with a price: therefore glorify God in your body, and in your spirit, which are God's."

The church is referred to as the bride. The bride then is made up of the universal body of believers, of believers from every land and every culture. According to Scripture, the bride is purchased by Christ. Jesus paid for the church with His own precious blood. His blood is the bride's eternal dowry. Therefore, every believer, who makes up the bride, has been bought by the blood of our Lord Christ Jesus.

Not only has the bride been purchased by Christ, but she is also espoused to Christ. In the eastern custom of marriage, the bride is espoused to her husband after her family pays a dowry. A dowry might also be a gift from the husband to his bride as well. An espousal is an agreement to marriage. The espousal period may last for as long as one year. During the espousal time, the couple do not come together and live as husband and wife. This is seen with Mary and Joseph who were the earthly parents of Jesus. They were espoused but not married. Mary became with child because of the supernatural work of the Holy Spirit.

Acts 20:28

"Take heed therefore unto yourselves, and to all the flock, over the which the Holy Ghost hath made you overseers, to feed the church of God, which he hath purchased with his own blood."

Luke 1:34-35

"Then said Mary unto the angel, How shall this be, seeing I know not a man? And the angel answered and said unto her, The Holy Ghost shall come upon thee, and the power of the Highest shall overshadow thee: there-

fore also that holy thing which shall be born of thee shall be called the Son of God."

Similarly, the bride is espoused to Christ. She is awaiting the return of her groom.

<u>2 Corinthians 11:2</u>

"For I am jealous over you with godly jealousy: for I have espoused you to one husband, that I may present you as a chaste virgin to Christ."

The bride of Christ is the church. The bride is purchased by Christ and the bride is espoused to Christ. A further relationship that the bride has with Christ is that one day He will return for His bride. Our Lord Christ Jesus, who is the groom, will one day return for His espoused bride.

<u>Revelation 21:9</u>

"And there came unto me one of the seven angels which had the seven vials full of the seven last plagues, and talked with me, saying, Come hither, I will show thee the bride, the Lamb's wife."

<u>Revelation 22:17</u>

"And the Spirit and the bride say, Come. And let him that heareth say, Come. And let him that is athirst come. And whosoever will, let him take the water of life freely."

When the Lord Christ Jesus comes for His bride the espousal period will come to an end and the marriage ceremony will take place. What a glorious moment when the saints who make up the congregation of the faithful are joined to Christ in marriage. At that moment the righteous acts of the saints will make up the wedding garment or fine linen which is worn by the bride.

<u>*Revelation 19:7-9*</u>

"Let us be glad and rejoice, and give honor to him: for the marriage of the Lamb is come, and his wife hath made herself ready. And to her was granted that she should be arrayed in fine linen, clean and white: for the fine linen is the righteousness of saints. And he saith unto me, Write, Blessed are they which are called unto the marriage supper of the Lamb. And he saith unto me, These are the true sayings of God."

REVIEW

What is the meaning of the word "ecclesiology"?

Ecclesiology means the study or doctrine of the church.

What is the meaning of the word "church"?

The word church means called out company or assembly.

What are the four different usages of the word "church"?

The four usages of the word church are:

- A local assembly
- Local assemblies
- The body of believers in a local setting
- The complete body of Christ

What are the meanings of the church?

The meanings of the church are as follows:

- The church is a mystery.
- The church is the body of which Christ is the head.
- The church is a spiritual building or house.
- The church is the bride of Christ.

Define the word "mystery" as used in the Scripture?

The word "mystery" means a truth revealed for the first time.

What verses support the scriptural definition of the word "mystery"?

The verses which support the scriptural definition of the word mystery are Ephesians 3:3-9.

What is the mystery which is being revealed at this present time?

The mystery is the Gospel message, that is, that anyone can become a child of God through faith in Jesus Christ as his personal Savior.

What is Christ's relationship with the church?

Christ is head of the church. He died that men might become members of His universal church.

What is the primary purpose of the church?

The primary or main purpose of the church is to glorify Christ through revealing Him to the unsaved world.

How is the revelation of Christ accomplished?

It is accomplished through the proclamation of the Gospel message and the teaching of Scriptures.

The church has been revealed as a spiritual building. What is the foundation of this building?

The foundation of this building is the apostles and prophets.

Who is the chief cornerstone of this foundation and building?

Jesus Christ is the chief cornerstone.

What is the bride's dowry?

The bride's dowry is the blood of Christ Jesus.

What is Christ's relationship with the bride?

Jesus Christ is the groom.

What future event will take place between the bride and the groom?

In the future Christ Jesus will come for His bride.

When the groom comes for His bride what will make up the wedding garment?

The works of the saints make up the wedding garment (Rev. 19:7-9).

C. Spiritual Gifts in the Church

What is a spiritual gift? A spiritual gift is a God-given ability for service. The word gift indicates that which is given by God's grace. Our Father is the donor. These spiritual abilities can function any place and any time. Three scriptural passages which show the spiritual gifts are as follows:

<u>Romans 12:3-8</u>

> *"For I say, through the grace given unto me, to every man that is among you, not to think of himself more highly than he ought to think; but to think soberly, according as God hath dealt to every man the measure of faith. For as we have many members in one body, and all members have not the same office: So we, being many, are one body in Christ, and every one members one of another. Having then gifts differing according to the grace that is given to us, whether prophecy, let us prophesy according to the proportion of faith; Or ministry, let us wait on our ministering: or he that teacheth, on teaching; Or he that*

> exhorteth, on exhortation: he that giveth, let him do it with simplicity; he that ruleth, with diligence; he that showeth mercy, with cheerfulness."

<u>1 Corinthians 12:28-31</u>

> "And God hath set some in the church, first apostles, secondarily prophets, thirdly teachers, after that miracles, then gifts of healings, helps, governments, diversities of tongues. Are all apostles? are all prophets? are all teachers? are all workers of miracles? Have all the gifts of healing? do all speak with tongues? do all interpret? But covet earnestly the best gifts: and yet show I unto you a more excellent way."

<u>Ephesians 4:11</u>

> "And he gave some, apostles; and some, prophets; and some, evangelists; and some, pastors and teachers."

The Word of God tells us that there are three primary purposes for the spiritual gifts. First, the gifts are to equip the saints for ministry.

<u>Ephesians 4:12a</u>

> "For the perfecting of the saints, for the work of the ministry..."

Secondly, the gifts are to edify the body of Christ. The word "edify" means to lift up or to encourage.

Ephesians 4:12b

"...for the edifying of the body of Christ."

The third purpose for spiritual gifts is to glorify Christ. Whatever we do we are exhorted to do it all to the glory of God.

1 Corinthians 10:31

"Whether therefore ye eat, or drink, or whatsoever ye do, do all to the glory of God."

Through those divine abilities given by God, saints are prepared and empowered for work. This work is the work of the church. Three primary functions of the church are to reveal Christ Jesus; to share the Gospel message and to teach the Scriptures. Remember that whatever we do we have to do it all to the glory of God.

D. The Spiritual Gifts to Believers

1. The Gift of Apostleship

Galatians 1:15-16

"But when it pleased God, who separated me from my mother's womb, and called me by his grace, To reveal his Son in me, that I might preach him among the heathen; immediately I conferred not with flesh and blood."

The word apostle means one who is sent. It is the sense of being a missionary.

Example: In the book of Galatians Paul wrote about his calling by God. He shows that God sent him to preach to the Gentiles. The word Gentiles means everyone who is not a Jew.

Special Sense: Paul was an apostle. In his apostleship he received direct inspiration from God to write the Holy Scriptures. After the Bible was complete God is no longer calling apostles as writers of His inspired word. We are warned by God that no one should add to His Word (Rev. 22:18; Deut. 4:2, 12:32; Prov. 30:6). Peter, John and all of the other New Testament writers were apostles called for this special purpose of writing God's inspired word.

Revelation 22:18

"For I testify unto every man that heareth the words of the prophecy of this book, If any man shall add unto these things, God shall add unto him the plagues that are written in this book."

Deuteronomy. 4:2

"Ye shall not add unto the word which I command you, neither shall ye diminish ought from it, that ye may keep the commandments of the Lord your God which I command you."

Deuteronomy 12:32

"What thing soever I command you, observe to do it: thou shalt not add thereto, nor diminish from it."

Proverbs 30:6

"Add thou not unto his words, lest he reprove thee, and thou be found a liar."

2. The Gift of Prophecy

The word prophecy means to preach or proclaim things to come.

Example: In the book of Acts we read about Agabus, a prophet who prophesied that there will be a worldwide famine.

Acts 11:27-28

"And in these days came prophets from Jerusalem unto Antioch. And there stood up one of them named Agabus, and signified by the Spirit that there should be great dearth throughout all the world: which came to pass in the days of Claudius Caesar."

Another example is when Philip's four daughters prophesied.

Acts 21:8-9

"And the next day we that were of Paul's company departed, and came unto Caesarea: and we entered into the house of Philip the evangelist, which was one of the seven; and abode with him. And the same man had four daughters, virgins, which did prophesy."

<u>Special Sense</u>: John the writer of Revelation was a prophet. He received God's inspired word by the leading of the Holy Spirit. Like the other apostles there is no one called today to write any new inspired word.

Revelation 1:3-4

"Blessed is he that readeth, and they that hear the words of this prophecy, and keep those things which are written therein: for the time is at hand. John to the seven churches which are in Asia: Grace be unto you, and peace, from him which is, and which was, and which is to come; and from the seven Spirits which are before his throne."

3. The Gifts of Miracles and Healing

These gifts are the ability to perform special acts.
<u>Example</u>: One example of the miracles is found in Acts 3 where Peter, in the name of Jesus, healed the man who was lame.

Acts 3:2-9

"And a certain man lame from his mother's womb was carried, whom they laid daily at the gate of the temple which is called Beautiful, to ask alms of them that entered into the temple; Who seeing Peter and John about to go into the temple asked an alms. And Peter, fastening his eyes upon him with John, said, Look on us. And he gave heed unto them, expecting to receive something of them. Then Peter said, Silver and gold have I none;

> but such as I have give I thee: In the name of Jesus Christ of Nazareth rise up and walk. And he took him by the right hand, and lifted him up: and immediately his feet and ankle bones received strength. And he leaping up stood, and walked, and entered with them into the temple, walking, and leaping, and praising God. And all the people saw him walking and praising God."

<u>1 Corinthians 12:9</u>

> "To another faith by the same Spirit; to another the gifts of healing by the same Spirit."

<u>1 Corinthians 12:28</u>

> "And God hath set some in the church, first apostles, secondarily prophets, thirdly teachers, after that miracles, then gifts of healings, helps, governments, diversities of tongues."

Another example is where Paul's handkerchiefs and aprons were placed on the sick and their diseases left them and the evil spirits went out of them.

<u>Acts 19:11-12</u>

> "And God wrought special miracles by the hands of Paul: So that from his body were brought unto the sick handkerchiefs or aprons, and the diseases departed from them, and the evil spirits went out of them."

4. The Gift of Tongues

   Acts 2:3-6

   "And there appeared unto them cloven tongues like as of fire, and it sat upon each of them. And they were all filled with the Holy Ghost, and began to speak with other tongues, as the Spirit gave them utterance. And there were dwelling at Jerusalem Jews, devout men, out of every nation under heaven. Now when this was noised abroad, the multitude came together, and were confounded, because that every man heard them speak in his own language."

The word tongues mean the ability to speak in other languages.

Example: The first experience of speaking in tongues was seen in Acts 2. Here it was obvious that tongues were the actual languages unknown to the speakers but understood by the hearers.

The purposes of the gift of tongues are as follows:

First, the purpose of tongues is to evangelize or share the Gospel message to people of a different culture and language.

   Acts 2:4-6

   "And they were all filled with the Holy Ghost, and began to speak with other tongues, as the Spirit gave them utterance. And there were dwelling at Jerusalem Jews, devout men, out of every nation under heaven. Now when

> this was noised abroad, the multitude came together, and were confounded, because that every man heard them speak in his own language."

Acts 2:11b

> "... we do hear them speak in our tongues the wonderful works of God."

Secondly, the purpose of tongues is to be a sign to unbelievers.

1 Corinthians 14:22a

> "Wherefore tongues are for a sign, not to them that believe, but to them that believe not...."

5. The Gift of Evangelism

The word evangelism means to proclaim. What is being proclaimed is the Gospel message. The word gospel means good news. It is the good news that Jesus came and died for our sins. He was buried and rose again the third day.

1 Corinthians 15:3-4

> "For I delivered unto you first of all that which I also received, how that Christ died for our sins according to the scriptures; And that he was buried, and that he rose again the third day according to the scriptures."

Example: In the book of Acts we read about Philip the evangelist.

Acts 21:8

"And the next day we that were of Paul's company departed, and came unto Caesarea: and we entered into the house of Philip the evangelist, which was one of the seven; and abode with him."

In 2 Timothy 4:5, Paul gave the exhortation to do the work of an evangelist.

All believers are called to evangelize. Also in some special terms there are those who are given the gift of evangelism.

2 Timothy 4:5

"But watch thou in all things, endure afflictions, do the work of an evangelist, make full proof of thy ministry."

In the book of Ephesians, we see where God gave some this gift of being an evangelist.

Ephesians 4:11

"And he gave some, apostles; and some, prophets; and some, evangelists; and some, pastors and teachers."

6. The Gift of Pastor

The word "pastor" means "to shepherd or protect." This gift is mentioned in Ephesians 4:11.

Ephesians 4:11

"And he gave some, apostles; and some, prophets; and some, evangelists; and some, pastors and teachers."

<u>Example</u>: In the book of Acts, Paul exhorts the pastors to take heed as they fulfill their ministry of pastoring or being a shepherd.

Acts 20:28

"Take heed therefore unto yourselves, and to all the flock, over the which the Holy Ghost hath made you overseers, to feed the church of God, which he hath purchased with his own blood."

1 Peter 5:2

"Feed the flock of God which is among you, taking the oversight thereof, not by constraint, but willingly; not for filthy lucre, but of a ready mind."

7. The Gift of Teaching

The one who has this gift is called to teach God's Word. All pastors have the gift of teaching, but not all teachers are pastors.

Romans 12:6-7

"Having then gifts differing according to the grace that is given to us, whether prophecy,

> let us prophesy according to the proportion of faith; Or ministry, let us wait on our ministering: or he that teacheth, on teaching."

Example: In 1st Timothy, Paul said that one of the abilities of deacons is to be able to teach.

> <u>1 Timothy 3:2</u>
>
> "A bishop then must be blameless, the husband of one wife, vigilant, sober, of good behavior, given to hospitality, apt to teach."

In Colossians, Paul said that he is laboring in teaching men in all wisdom.

> <u>Colossians 1:28-29</u>
>
> "Whom we preach, warning every man, and teaching every man in all wisdom; that we may present every man perfect in Christ Jesus: Whereunto I also labor, striving according to his working, which worketh in me mightily."

8. The Gift of Exhortation

The word exhortation has a three-fold meaning:

- to encourage
- to comfort, and
- to admonish or lift up

> <u>Romans 12:8a</u>
>
> "Or he that exhorteth, on exhortation..."

Example: Paul encourages the saints in First Timothy to give attention to the ministry of exhortation.

1 Timothy 4:13

"Till I come, give attendance to reading, to exhortation, to doctrine."

9. The Gift of Giving

Those who have this gift are encouraged to give with liberality.

Romans 12:8b

"...he that giveth, let him do it with simplicity..."

Example: In the book of Acts, we read where our Lord Jesus said that it is more blessed to give than to receive.

Acts 20:35

"I have showed you all things, how that so laboring ye ought to support the weak, and to remember the words of the Lord Jesus, how he said, It is more blessed to give than to receive."

10. The Gift of Leading

This is the same as shepherding. It means that the person with this gift will give direction using God's Word as his guide. In general issues the Holy Spirit will give him wisdom to lead.

Romans 12:8c

"...he that ruleth, with diligence..."

<u>Example</u>: In the book of Hebrews the writer encourages believers to submit to those who rule. This word rule means to lead. It refers to the leaders of the church.

Hebrews 13:7

"Remember them which have the rule over you, who have spoken unto you the Word of God: whose faith follow, considering the end of their conversation."

Hebrews 13:17

"Obey them that have the rule over you, and submit yourselves: for they watch for your souls, as they that must give account, that they may do it with joy, and not with grief: for that is unprofitable for you."

11. The Gift of Mercy

The word mercy means to have pity or compassion. It is to feel sympathy with the misery of another. Saints who have this gift are very tender hearted.
<u>Example</u>: Paul exhorts the believers at Colossia to exercise this gift of mercy.

Colossians 3:12

"Put on therefore, as the elect of God, holy and beloved, bowels of mercies, kindness, humbleness of mind, meekness, long-suffering."

REVIEW

What is a spiritual gift?

A spiritual gift is a God-given ability for service.

What are the three primary purposes for the spiritual gifts?

They are:

- to equip the saints for ministry
- to edify or encourage each other
- to glorify our Lord Christ Jesus

Who gives the gifts to saints?

God distributes the gifts as is pleasing to Him.

What is the meaning of the word "apostle"?

The word apostle means one who is sent.

What makes the apostleship of Paul and the other New Testament writers different from other apostles?

They were apostles who received the special ability to write God's Word. They wrote as the Holy Spirit led.

What is the meaning of the term to "prophecy"?

The term prophecy means to proclaim, or to preach.

Give a New Testament example where women functioned under the gift of prophecy?

In Acts 21:8-9, Philip, the evangelist, had four daughters who were virgins who did prophesy.

What is the meaning of the word "evangelize"?

The word evangelize means to proclaim the Gospel message.

What is the meaning of the word "pastor"?

The word pastor refers to one who shepherds or protects.

What is the meaning of the word "exhortation"?

Exhortation means to encourage, to comfort or to lift up.

What should be the heart attitude of the one who gives?

The one who gives should do so with a cheerful heart.

Who in the church will demonstrate the gift of leading?

Church leaders such as pastors, deacons, and elders will demonstrate the gift of leading. Believers other than church leaders may also have the gift to lead.

Who empowers the believer to function under any of the gifts?

The Holy Spirit empowers believers.

E. The Church Ordinances

There are two church ordinances: baptism and the Lord's Supper. Baptism usually takes place not long after salvation. The believer experiences two types of baptism. They are spiritual baptism and water baptism. The Lord's Supper is taken all during the believer's life.

1. Baptism

The word baptism means to dip or to immerse. Therefore, baptism does not mean sprinkling.

a. The Lord commanded baptism.

All believers are commanded to be baptized. Therefore, as believers we do not have a choice. We all have to submit ourselves to God's command. Baptism is not something to pray about since it is God's will for all believers to be baptized. The believer must obey God's command.

Matthew 28:18-20

"And Jesus came and spake unto them, saying, All power is given unto me in heaven and in earth. Go ye therefore, and teach all nations, baptizing them in the name of the Father, and of the Son, and of the Holy Ghost: Teaching them to observe all things whatsoever I have

commanded you: and, lo, I am with you alway, even unto the end of the world. Amen."

b. Significance of Baptism

By baptism the believer is declaring publicly his faith in Christ Jesus as his Lord and Savior. Baptism is also an outward demonstration of an inward act, and symbolizes the death, burial and resurrection of our Lord Christ Jesus.

<u>Colossians 2:12</u>

"Buried with him in baptism, wherein also ye are risen with him through the faith of the operation of God, who hath raised him from the dead."

<u>2 Corinthians 5:14</u>

"For the love of Christ constraineth us; because we thus judge, that if one died for all, then were all dead."

It is important to understand that baptism is not a saving ordinance. Salvation is only possible through faith in our Lord Christ Jesus.

<u>Ephesians 2:8-9</u>

"For by grace are ye saved through faith; and that not of yourselves: it is the gift of God: Not of works, lest any man should boast."

2. The Lord's Supper

The second ordinance given by God to the church is the partaking of the elements which symbolizes the Lord's Supper.

a. Factors Relevant to the Lord's Supper

The Lord's Supper took place on the same night our Lord was betrayed.

> *1 Corinthians 11:23*
>
> *"For I have received of the Lord that which also I delivered unto you, That the Lord Jesus the same night in which he was betrayed took bread."*
>
> *In the Lord's Supper, the element which is eaten represents Christ's body and the drink represents His blood. These elements do not become the actual body and blood of our Lord. They serve only as a remembrance.*
>
> *1 Corinthians 11:24-25*
>
> *"And when he had given thanks, he brake it, and said, Take, eat: this is my body, which is broken for you: this do in remembrance of me. After the same manner also he took the cup, when he had supped, saying, This cup is the new testament in my blood: this do ye, as oft as ye drink it, in remembrance of me."*

Whenever we partake of the Lord's Supper, we are proclaiming His death until He calls His church home.

> *1 Corinthians 11:26*
>
> *"For as often as ye eat this bread, and drink this cup, ye do show the Lord's death till he come."*

The believer renews his fellowship whenever he partakes of the Lord's Supper. This is done because God commands us to examine ourselves and to confess our sins.

> *1 Corinthians 11:27-28*
>
> *"Wherefore whosoever shall eat this bread, and drink this cup of the Lord, unworthily, shall be guilty of the body and blood of the Lord. But let a man examine himself, and so let him eat of that bread, and drink of that cup."*

Like water baptism the Lord's Supper will not save anyone. Salvation is only through faith in our Lord Christ Jesus.

REVIEW

What are the two church ordinances?

They are baptism and communion.

What is the meaning of the word "ordinance"?

The word ordinance is that which has been commanded for believers to practice.

What does baptism signify?

The significance of baptism is as follows:

- The believer's faith in Christ Jesus as Lord and Savior
- The death, burial and resurrection of our Lord
- Our position in Christ

What do the elements of the Lord's Supper symbolize?

The elements symbolize the body and blood of our Lord.

What are we proclaiming as we partake of the Lord's Supper?

We are proclaiming our Lord's death.

Does baptism or the Lord's Supper bring salvation?

Neither of the ordinances provides salvation.

Chapter 5

THE DOCTRINE OF SATAN AND DEMONS

A. The Origin of Satan

Satan's name was Lucifer. The word "Lucifer" means "son of the morning." Lucifer was created by God. He was created in perfect beauty.

> *Ezekiel 28:11-12*
>
> *"Moreover the word of the Lord came unto me, saying, Son of man, take up a lamentation upon the king of Tyrus, and say unto him, Thus saith the Lord God; Thou sealest up the sum, full of wisdom, and perfect in beauty."*
>
> *Ezekiel 28:15*
>
> *"Thou wast perfect in thy ways from the day that thou wast created, till iniquity was found in thee."*

Satan was a master musician in heaven. This was before his fall. However, today, we can see in the world how Satan uses music to control the souls of men.

Ezekiel 28:13c

"... the workmanship of thy tabrets and of thy pipes was prepared in thee in the day that thou wast created."

In time, Lucifer became prideful. This pride was the root cause of his fall. After his fall, his name was changed from Lucifer to Satan. The name Satan means adversary, hater, and accuser.

Isaiah 14:12-15

"How art thou fallen from heaven, O Lucifer, son of the morning! how art thou cut down to the ground, which didst weaken the nations! For thou hast said in thine heart, I will ascend into heaven, I will exalt my throne above the stars of God: I will sit also upon the mount of the congregation, in the sides of the north: I will ascend above the heights of the clouds; I will be like the most High. Yet thou shalt be brought down to hell, to the sides of the pit."

The sin of pride caused Satan's fall. He desires to be above God. He said in his heart, "I will" which reflects his desire for his own glory. Today, he is still filling men's hearts with this sin of pride. Apostle Paul warns the church not to place a novice into a leadership position. This could lead to pride. The end result will be condemnation like Satan.

1 Timothy 3:6

"Not a novice, lest being lifted up with pride he fall into the condemnation of the devil."

REVIEW

What was Satan's name before his fall?

His name was Lucifer.

What is the meaning of the name Lucifer?

The name Lucifer means "son of the morning".

What was the chief reason for Satan's fall?

The chief reason for Satan's fall was pride.

How do we know that Satan was a musician in heaven?

He was the chief angel. The workmanship of timbrels and pipes were prepared for him on the day he was created.

What is the meaning of the name Satan?

The name Satan means adversary, hater, and accuser.

What was Paul's warning concerning church leadership?

Apostle Paul warned that a novice or immature believer should not be put in a leadership position. Such quick placement may lead to pride.

B. Names and Descriptive Titles of Satan

1. Satan

   1 Peter 5:8-9

   "Be sober, be vigilant; because your adversary the devil, as a roaring lion, walketh about, seeking whom he may devour."

This name means adversary.

2. Devil

   Revelation 12:9-10

   "And the great dragon was cast out, that old serpent, called the Devil, and Satan, which deceiveth the whole world: he was cast out into the earth, and his angels were cast out with him. And I heard a loud voice saying in heaven, Now is come salvation, and strength, and the kingdom of our God, and the power of his Christ: for the accuser of our brethren is cast down, which accused them before our God day and night."

This name means accuser or deceiver.

3. Beelzebub

   Matthew 12:24

   "But when the Pharisees heard it, they said, This fellow doth not cast out devils, but by Beelzebub the prince of the devils."

   Mark 3:22

   "And the scribes which came down from Jerusalem said, He hath Beelzebub, and by the prince of the devils casteth he out devils."

   Luke 11:18

   "If Satan also be divided against himself, how shall his kingdom stand? Because ye say that I cast out devils through Beelzebub."

This name means ruler of demons.

4. Belial

   2 Corinthians 6:15

   "And what concord hath Christ with Belial? or what part hath he that believeth with an infidel?"

This name refers to Satan.

5. The wicked one

1 John 2:14b

"...I have written unto you, young men, because ye are strong, and the Word of God abideth in you, and ye have overcome the wicked one."

Satan is the wicked one. His deeds are always evil. His desire is to destroy. He is the devil.

6. Ruler of this world

1 John 2:16 -17

"For all that is in the world, the lust of the flesh, and the lust of the eyes, and the pride of life, is not of the Father, but is of the world. And the world passeth away, and the lust thereof: but he that doeth the will of God abideth for ever."

John 14:30

"Hereafter I will not talk much with you: for the prince of this world cometh, and hath nothing in me."

Satan is the ruler of this world. This world of evil is a well-organized system. This world offers lust and pride. This world is not of our heavenly Father. This world and all its evil will pass away.

Satan controls this world as ruler. He does so through his network of demons.

7. The god of this age

   2 Corinthians 4:4

   "In whom the god of this world hath blinded the minds of them which believe not, lest the light of the glorious gospel of Christ, who is the image of God, should shine unto them."

This title refers to Satan. He is lord over this wicked age. Satan, who is the god of this age, blinds the hearts of men from responding to the Gospel.

8. Prince of the power of the air

   Ephesians 2:2

   "Wherein in time past ye walked according to the course of this world, according to the prince of the power of the air, the spirit that now worketh in the children of disobedience:"

In the above verse both words, prince and spirit refer to Satan.

9. The old serpent

   Revelation 12:9

   "And the great dragon was cast out, that old serpent, called the Devil, and Satan, which deceiveth the whole world: he was cast out into the earth, and his angels were cast out with him."

10. Accuser of the brethren

Revelation 12:10

"And I heard a loud voice saying in heaven, Now is come salvation, and strength, and the kingdom of our God, and the power of his Christ: for the accuser of our brethren is cast down, which accused them before our God day and night."

Satan always accuses us before God. But, praise God, we are saved and cleansed by the blood of Christ Jesus our Lord. Our Father in heaven sees us as holy and without blame because of what Christ did for us.

11. Angel of light

2 Corinthians 11:13-14

"For such are false apostles, deceitful workers, transforming themselves into the apostles of Christ. And no marvel; for Satan himself is transformed into an angel of light."

Satan transforms himself into an angel of light so that he may deceive people into believing his lies. Many use the name of our Lord Christ Jesus, but are really instruments of Satan. This is why God's children have to be aware of the spirits that are working against them.

12. Father of lies

   John 8:44

   "Ye are of your father the devil, and the lusts of your father ye will do. He was a murderer from the beginning, and abode not in the truth, because there is no truth in him. When he speaketh a lie, he speaketh of his own: for he is a liar, and the father of it."

   Lies and deceit started with Satan. Jesus said he was a liar from the very beginning. Believers have to be especially careful today, for Satan uses men with evil hearts to lie and deceive many.

13. Murderer

   John 8:44

   "...He was a murderer from the beginning, and abode not in the truth, because there is no truth in him."

   Satan wants to murder or destroy God's children. Praise God that he cannot harm us apart from God's permissive will. The devil knows that he must destroy God's children in order to keep this world in darkness.

   John 10:10

   "The thief cometh not, but for to steal, and to kill, and to destroy: I am come that they might have life, and that they might have it more abundantly."

14. Roaring lion

1 Peter 5:8

"Be sober, be vigilant; because your adversary the devil, as a roaring lion, walketh about, seeking whom he may devour."

2 Timothy 1:7

"For God hath not given us the spirit of fear; but of power, and of love, and of a sound mind."

This title tells us that Satan's aim is to instill fear in the hearts of men. He knows that fear can cause God's children to stumble. The Bible, however, tells us that God did not give us a spirit of fear.

15. Ruler of darkness

Ephesians 6:12

"For we wrestle not against flesh and blood, but against principalities, against powers, against the rulers of the darkness of this world, against spiritual wickedness in high places."

This world is in darkness because of sin. Satan is the ruler of this worldly kingdom. He is lord over his network of demons that are trying to destroy the souls of men.

C. Satan's Limitations

Even though Satan is the ruler of this evil world order he has limitations.

> *Ezekiel 28:15*
>
> *"Thou wast perfect in thy ways from the day that thou wast created, till iniquity was found in thee."*

1. Satan is not omnipresent.

> *Luke 10:18*
>
> *"And he said unto them, I beheld Satan as lightning fall from heaven."*

Satan cannot be everywhere at the same time. Through his many demons, he is able to control events around the world. But he himself can only be at one place at a time.

2. Satan is not omnipotent

> *Job 1:12*
>
> *"And the Lord said unto Satan, Behold, all that he hath is in thy power; only upon himself put not forth thine hand. So Satan went forth from the presence of the Lord."*

Satan is subject to God's sovereign control. He has to obey God's Word. In the Book of Job, Satan could not harm Job without God's permissive will. God allowed Satan to inflict pain on Job in order that God may show His compassion and mercy. This is comforting to us because we know that Satan cannot win any battles over us. Our God reigns. Satan has been defeated. Our Lord Jesus is Lord and Master of our lives.

   3. Satan can be resisted by Christians.

James 4:7

"Submit yourselves therefore to God. Resist the devil, and he will flee from you."

<u>Ephesians 6:16</u>

"Above all, taking the shield of faith, wherewith ye shall be able to quench all the fiery darts of the wicked."

The person who is born again has been sealed with the Holy Spirit. Jesus has already won the victory on Calvary's tree. Through the power of the blood of Christ, Satan's attacks can be defeated. The believer's shield is his faith in Christ Jesus as Lord.

REVIEW

What is the meaning of the name "devil"?

The name devil means accuser or deceiver.

What is the meaning of the name "Beelzebub"?

The name Beelzebub means ruler of demons.

How can we overcome the wicked one?

We can overcome the wicked one by the Word of God.

What are the three elements of this world?

They are the lust of the flesh; the lust of the eyes, and the pride of life.

How does Satan control this world?

He controls this world through his army of demons.

What kind of spirit does the believer have?

The believer has been given a spirit of power, of love and of a sound mind.

In what ways is Satan limited?

Satan is limited in the following ways:

- He is not omniscient.
- He is not omnipresent.
- He is not omnipotent.

What is the believers' shield against Satan's attacks?

The believers' shield against Satan's attacks is his faith in the Lord Christ Jesus.

D. The Work of Satan

Satan and his demons are working towards blinding the minds of unbelievers. Satan does not want people to be saved. He knows that his final judgment is certain, therefore he is trying to deceive as many as he can to also suffer eternal condemnation.

<u>2 Corinthians 4:3-4</u>

"But if our gospel be hid, it is hid to them that are lost: In whom the god of this world hath blinded the minds of them which believe not, lest the light of the glorious gospel of Christ, who is the image of God, should shine unto them."

1. Satan snatches the Word from the hearts of unbelievers.

   <u>Luke 8:12</u>

   "Those by the way side are they that hear; then cometh the devil, and taketh away the word out of their hearts, lest they should believe and be saved."

Satan knows that the Gospel message is the only means that can bring eternal life. Through the Word of God, man can reject Satan's kingdom and accept Christ Jesus as Lord and Savior. Thus, when the word is proclaimed, Satan will try to take it away from the heart of men before they can believe.

Mark 4:15

"And these are they by the way side, where the word is sown; but when they have heard, Satan cometh immediately, and taketh away the word that was sown in their hearts."

12. Satan uses unbelievers to oppose God's work.

Revelation 2:9

"I know thy works, and tribulation, and poverty, (but thou art rich) and I know the blasphemy of them which say they are Jews, and are not, but are the synagogue of Satan."

Unbelievers can be very selfish. Satan works through unbelievers to live for their own selfish desires instead of serving God.

3. Satan tempts men to lie.

Acts 5:3

"But Peter said, Ananias, why hath Satan filled thine heart to lie to the Holy Ghost, and to keep back part of the price of the land?"

In the book of Acts, we see Satan filling Ananias' heart to lie. Ananias kept back what he was to give to God. This cost him his life.

4. Satan is always accusing Christians.

> *Revelation 12:10*
>
> *"And I heard a loud voice saying in heaven, Now is come salvation, and strength, and the kingdom of our God, and the power of his Christ: for the accuser of our brethren is cast down, which accused them before our God day and night."*

He is the false accuser. He slanders believers. However, praise God, we are kept under the blood of Christ. Our Lord Jesus has washed us from all unrighteousness. We are eternally secure in Christ. Above all, our Heavenly Father sees us holy and without blame.

5. Satan hinders the Christian work.

> *1 Thessalonians 2:17-18*
>
> *"But we, brethren, being taken from you for a short time in presence, not in heart, endeavored the more abundantly to see your face with great desire. Wherefore we would have come unto you, even I Paul, once and again; but Satan hindered us."*

There were times when Satan hindered Paul's work. Believers have to be alert about Satan's attacks. We are indeed in a spiritual warfare.

6. Satan sends his demons to attempt to defeat Christians.

Ephesians 6:11-12

"Put on the whole armor of God, that ye may be able to stand against the wiles of the devil. For we wrestle not against flesh and blood, but against principalities, against powers, against the rulers of the darkness of this world, against spiritual wickedness in high places."

The Bible tells us that Satan has an order or network for his army. He is well organized. He has different levels of demonic forces.

7. Satan tempts men to commit acts of immorality.

1 Corinthians 7:5

"Defraud ye not one the other, except it be with consent for a time, that ye may give yourselves to fasting and prayer; and come together again, that Satan tempt you not for your incontinency."

God warns believers to safeguard against Satan's attacks in their marriage. Husbands and wives should maintain a close relationship at all times. This prevents Satan from exploiting marital discord as an avenue of attack.

8. Satan works through wicked men to hinder men from becoming saved.

   Matthew 13:36-39

   "Then Jesus sent the multitude away, and went into the house: and his disciples came unto him, saying, Declare unto us the parable of the tares of the field. He answered and said unto them, He that soweth the good seed is the Son of man; The field is the world; the good seed are the children of the kingdom; but the tares are the children of the wicked one; The enemy that sowed them is the devil; the harvest is the end of the world; and the reapers are the angels."

9. Satan incites persecution against Christians.

   2 Timothy 3:11-12

   "Persecutions, afflictions, which came unto me at Antioch, at Iconium, at Lystra; what persecutions I endured: but out of them all the Lord delivered me. Yea, and all that will live godly in Christ Jesus shall suffer persecution."

The Bible tells us that those who desire to live godly in Christ will suffer persecution. Praise God that He always delivers us and gives us the victory.

REVIEW

What is Satan's final judgment?

Satan knows that he and all evil spirits will be cast into eternal hell.

Name one way in which Satan opposes God's work?

One way that Satan opposes God's work is through the selfish desires of unbelievers.

Why is Satan called the accuser?

Satan is called the accuser because he accuses believers night and day before God.

How are we to stand against Satan's attacks?

We are to stand against Satan's attacks by putting on the whole armor of God.

Who are we fighting this spiritual battle against?

We are not fighting against men. We are fighting against principalities, against powers, against the rulers of the darkness of this age, against spiritual hosts of wickedness in high places.

What word of assurance do we have as we suffer persecution?

We have the assurance that God will deliver us. Furthermore, our Lord Jesus promises us that He is always with us.

E. The Origin of Demons

Satan has his army of demons. Where did the demons come from? The Bible tells us that there was a war in heaven. Michael, God's angel, and his angels fought against Satan and his angels which are demons. Demons were not created by Satan. They were created by God. They were created in holiness. When Satan became prideful and sinned he deceived many angels to follow him. These angels were cast out of heaven with Satan. In this fallen state they are now called demons.

Revelation 12:7-9

"And there was war in heaven: Michael and his angels fought against the dragon; and the dragon fought and his angels, And prevailed not; neither was their place found any more in heaven. And the great dragon was cast out, that old serpent, called the Devil, and Satan, which deceiveth the whole world: he was cast out into the earth, and his angels were cast out with him."

2 Peter 2:4-6

"For if God spared not the angels that sinned, but cast them down to hell, and delivered them into chains of darkness, to be reserved unto judgment; And spared not the old world, but saved Noah the eighth person, a preacher of righteousness, bringing in the flood upon the world of the ungodly; And turning the cities of Sodom and Gomorrah into ashes condemned them with an overthrow, making them an

example unto those that after should live ungodly."

In the above verse, we see that there is no salvation for the fallen angels. They have been appointed a day of assured judgment. Our Lord Jesus did not die for the fallen angels. He died for mankind.

<u>Jude 1:6</u>

"And the angels which kept not their first estate, but left their own habitation, he hath reserved in everlasting chains under darkness unto the judgment of the great day."

F. The Characteristics of Demons

<u>Matthew 12:24</u>

"But when the Pharisees heard it, they said, This fellow doth not cast out devils, but by Beelzebub the prince of the devils."

Satan is referred to as the prince of demons. Not all demons are chained for judgment. Many demons under Satan's command are doing his evil works in the world.

Beelzebub is another name for Satan. It is a title for the "lord of the flies." Satan is then referred to as the ruler of the demons. Demons are foul or evil spirits. Let us now examine the characteristics of demons.

1. Demons are spirit beings.

   Mark 9:25

   "When Jesus saw that the people came running together, he rebuked the foul spirit, saying unto him, Thou dumb and deaf spirit, I charge thee, come out of him, and enter no more into him."

2. Demons are intellectual beings.

   a. They knew Jesus.

   Mark 1:23-24

   "And there was in their synagogue a man with an unclean spirit; and he cried out, Saying, Let us alone; what have we to do with thee, thou Jesus of Nazareth? art thou come to destroy us? I know thee who thou art, the Holy One of God."

Since these demons were created by our Lord Christ Jesus before their fall they recognized Jesus as the Holy One of God.

   b. Demons also know that there is only one true God.

   James 2:19

   "Thou believest that there is one God; thou doest well: the devils also believe, and tremble."

c. Demons also have a satanic doctrine of their own.

1 Timothy 4:1

"Now the Spirit speaketh expressly, that in the latter times some shall depart from the faith, giving heed to seducing spirits, and doctrines of devils."

The doctrines or teachings of demons are everywhere today. In many churches false teachings are growing. The Bible tells us that Satan appears as an angel of light and deceives many. Increasingly, we see many churches spending less time studying the Bible and more time on worldly philosophies.

d. Demons know of their own doom.

Matthew 8:29

"And, behold, they cried out, saying, What have we to do with thee, Jesus, thou Son of God? art thou come hither to torment us before the time?"

Satan and his demons know that God has appointed for them a day of judgment and eternal condemnation. This is why they are working diligently to lead as many people to this same condemnation. Jesus has provided salvation for mankind, not for demons.

3. Demons are fallen angels.

They were created by God and were holy before their fall. Their fall came when they followed Satan.

REVIEW

Who is the prince of demons?

Satan is the prince of demons.

What are the characteristics of demons?

Demons are spiritual and intellectual beings.

G. The Work of Demons

1. Demons oppose the purpose of God.

    <u>Revelation 16:13-14</u>

    "And I saw three unclean spirits like frogs come out of the mouth of the dragon, and out of the mouth of the beast, and out of the mouth of the false prophet. For they are the spirits of devils, working miracles, which go forth unto the kings of the earth and of the whole world, to gather them to the battle of that great day of God Almighty."

2. Demons can inflict diseases.

    <u>Matthew 9:33</u>

    "And when the devil was cast out, the dumb spake: and the multitudes marveled, saying, It was never so seen in Israel."

3. Demons can possess men.

Matthew 4:24

"And his fame went throughout all Syria: and they brought unto him all sick people that were taken with divers diseases and torments, and those which were possessed with devils, and those which were lunatic, and those that had the palsy; and he healed them."

H. The Characteristics of Demon Possession

The word possession means to control or to reside in. Demons can come within someone and take control. A person must open his soul for possession to take place. This means giving place for the devil to exert strong influence. For example, if someone opens his heart to the world of Satan worship, this can lead to possession. Satan worship may be in the form of listening to rock music, or getting involved in palm reading or psychic reading and all other cultic practices. When demons come into someone, they do not like to give up their possession. It takes a great deal of prayer and spiritual battle in order to experience deliverance from possession.

1. The demon-possessed may suffer physically.

Matthew 9:32-33

"As they went out, behold, they brought to him a dumb man possessed with a devil. And when the devil was cast out, the dumb spake: and the multitudes marveled, saying, It was never so seen in Israel."

2. The demon possessed may suffer mentally.

   Luke 8:27-29

   "And when he went forth to land, there met him out of the city a certain man, which had devils long time, and ware no clothes, neither abode in any house, but in the tombs. When he saw Jesus, he cried out, and fell down before him, and with a loud voice said, What have I to do with thee, Jesus, thou Son of God most high? I beseech thee, torment me not. (For he had commanded the unclean spirit to come out of the man. For oftentimes it had caught him: and he was kept bound with chains and in fetters; and he brake the bands, and was driven of the devil into the wilderness.)"

3. The demon-possessed may suffer from moral impurity.

   Mark 5:2

   "And when he was come out of the ship, immediately there met him out of the tombs a man with an unclean spirit."

4. The demon-possessed may be controlled by seducing spirits, and doctrines of demons.

   1 Timothy 4:1

   "Now the Spirit speaketh expressly, that in the latter times some shall depart from the faith,

giving heed to seducing spirits, and doctrines of devils."

I. The Destiny of Demons

The Bible teaches that demons like Satan are eternally condemned. The time will come when Satan and all the demons will be cast into the lake of fire eternally.

Matthew 25:41

"Then shall he say also unto them on the left hand, Depart from me, ye cursed, into everlasting fire, prepared for the devil and his angels."

2 Peter 2:4

"For if God spared not the angels that sinned, but cast them down to hell, and delivered them into chains of darkness, to be reserved unto judgment."

Jude 1:6

"And the angels which kept not their first estate, but left their own habitation, he hath reserved in everlasting chains under darkness unto the judgment of the great day."

REVIEW

What are the works of demons?

The works of demons are as follows:

> Demons oppose the purpose of God.
> Demons can inflict diseases.
> Demons can possess men.

What are the effects of demon possession?

The effects of demon possession are as follows:

> The demon-possessed may suffer physically.
> The demon-possessed may suffer mentally.
> The demon-possessed may suffer from moral impurity.
> The demon-possessed may be controlled by seducing spirits and doctrines of demons.

What is the destiny of demons?

Demons and Satan will be cast into the lake of fire eternally.

Chapter 6

THE DOCTRINE OF SALVATION

Salvation is the setting free or the state of being set free from the penalty of sin. It is the work God performs for and in every person who believes the Gospel of Jesus Christ. It also refers to the work of the Holy Spirit in a person whereby they become increasingly victorious over the practice of sin. It also refers to a future state for all believers wherein they are set free from the presence of sin. Salvation is based purely on God's amazing grace and is made possible by the death of Jesus Christ for the sins of the world.

Ephesians 1:7

> "In whom we have redemption through his blood, the forgiveness of sins, according to the riches of his grace."

A. The Need for Salvation

Romans 3:23

"For all have sinned, and come short of the glory of God."

This verse tells us that everyone is a sinner and fails to measure up to God's standard of righteousness. Sin has caused man to be eternally separated from God. It originated in the Garden of Eden when Adam and Eve disobeyed God. Our sins demonstrate that we fall short of the glory of God. To fall short of the glory of God means that man is no longer qualified to enter God's heaven.

1. Man's Hopeless State

   Romans 6:23

   "For the wages of sin is death; but the gift of God is eternal life through Jesus Christ our Lord."

   Isaiah 59:2

   "But your iniquities have separated between you and your God, and your sins have hid his face from you, that he will not hear."

In order for us to appreciate God's gracious work of salvation, it is necessary for us to first understand man's lost and hopeless state outside of Christ. Romans 6:23 tells us that the wages or penalty of sin is death. This means that we are eternally condemned because of sin. This death means both spiritual and physical death. Spiritual death is a state of broken fellowship with God. Isaiah 59:2 tells us that our sins have caused God to hide His face from us and to turn a deaf ear to our prayers. If a person were to die in a state of spiritual death, he would forever remain separated from God. Such a person would face the "second death" which is a lake of fire and brimstone. This place of eternal torment was originally prepared for Satan and his angels, but all who die and have not received salvation through Jesus Christ will be condemned there for all eternity.

2. The Nature of Sin

Sin is anything that demonstrates that we fall short of God's holiness. All disobedience to God's commands is sin. The Bible also tells us that anything not done through faith is sin. Sin also includes the failure to do good works. Even evil thoughts and desires that we might harbor in our minds and hearts is sin. Sin is a natural result of the sinful nature we inherited from Adam.

James 2:10

"For whosoever shall keep the whole law, and yet offend in one point, he is guilty of all."

God's law was given to man to be a yardstick for holy and righteous living. It demonstrates to man the holiness of God and the sinfulness of man. No one has been able to keep God's law perfectly. God is perfectly holy; not even one sin can be acceptable to Him. If a person disobeys any of God's laws, it proves that he is not holy and guilty under the law. The truth of the matter is that we are all repeat violators of God's laws.

Romans 5:19

"For as by one man's disobedience many were made sinners...."

The human race is condemned because of Adam's sin. All have inherited Adam's sinful nature since he is the father of all living. It is this that makes us sinners by nature and sinners by choice. Through his disobedience, Adam lost his perfect innocence and the fellowship he had with God. His very nature became corrupted. He became a sinner and received God's judgment of death. All who were born of Adam inherited this sin nature. Therefore, in Adam all were born under sin's curse.

3. The Results of Sin

Man is now under the Adamic curse. This fall of man took place in the Garden of Eden when Satan tempted Eve.

Genesis 3:1-5

"Now the serpent was more subtile than any beast of the field which the Lord God had made. And he said unto the woman, Yea, hath God said, Ye shall not eat of every tree of the garden? And the woman said unto the serpent, We may eat of the fruit of the trees of the garden: But of the fruit of the tree which is in the midst of the garden, God hath said, Ye shall not eat of it, neither shall ye touch it, lest ye die. And the serpent said unto the woman, Ye shall not surely die: For God doth know that in the day ye eat thereof, then your

eyes shall be opened, and ye shall be as gods, knowing good and evil."

Satan is the deceiver. He is a liar and has been described as the father of lies. He deceived Eve into thinking that God had not been fair since He restricted the eating of the fruit of one of the trees. Both Adam and Eve disobeyed God and ate of the forbidden fruit. Their sin was not merely eating the fruit, but disobeying God's command.

This act of disobedience caused man's relationship with God to be broken. When God created man he was perfect in nature. When man sinned, he lost this nature and broke his fellowship with God. Instead of fellowship, man is now under God's wrath.

<u>Romans 1:18</u>

"For the wrath of God is revealed from heaven against all ungodliness and unrighteousness of men, who hold the truth in unrighteousness."

<u>John 3:36</u>

"He that believeth on the Son hath everlasting life: and he that believeth not the Son shall not see life; but the wrath of God abideth on him."

REVIEW

What is salvation?

Salvation is the work of God by which the believer is set free from the penalty of sin. It also includes the continuing work of the Holy Spirit in setting the believer free from the practice of sin. It also refers to the final state of the believer in which he is set free from the presence of sin.

What is the consequence of sin upon man?

All men have been placed under the judgment of death because of sin. Death is both physical and spiritual.

What is sin?

Sin is disobedience to God's law. Anything not done in faith, failure to do good works, or harboring evil thoughts and desires is considered sin. It is a demonstration that we fall short of the glory of God.

How has sin affected man's fellowship with God?

Instead of fellowship with God, man is now under His wrath.

B. God's Remedy for Sin

Through Adam, sin and judgment came upon mankind. Through Jesus, the Son of God, eternal life has been provided for mankind.

> *1 Corinthians 15:21-22*
>
> *"For since by man came death, by man came also the resurrection of the dead. For as in Adam all die, even so in Christ shall all be made alive.*

Romans 5:19

"For as by one man's disobedience many were made sinners, so by the obedience of one shall many be made righteous."

1. Jesus became our substitute.

Jesus is holy and righteous. He was the only one qualified to become our substitute.

2 Corinthians 5:21

"For he hath made him to be sin for us, who knew no sin; that we might be made the righteousness of God in him."

Matthew 20:28

"Even as the Son of man came not to be ministered unto, but to minister, and to give his life a ransom for many."

The word "ransom" means in place of. Thus Jesus gave His life in place of or as a substitution for sinners.

2. Jesus' death provided redemption.

The word redemption has three root meanings. First, it means "to pay a price for something."

1 Corinthians 6:19-20

"What? know ye not that your body is the temple of the Holy Ghost which is in you,

> which ye have of God, and ye are not your own? For ye are bought with a price: therefore glorify God in your body, and in your spirit, which are God's."

The second meaning for the word redemption is to purchase out of a market.

Ephesians 1:7

> "In whom we have redemption through his blood, the forgiveness of sins, according to the riches of his grace."

The third meaning for the word redemption is "to loose." Thus, the sinner has been redeemed and loose or set free from the penalty of sin. The sinner is released or loose from sin through the shed blood of Christ Jesus.

Hebrews 9:11-12

> "But Christ being come an high priest of good things to come, by a greater and more perfect tabernacle, not made with hands, that is to say, not of this building; Neither by the blood of goats and calves, but by his own blood he entered in once into the holy place, having obtained eternal redemption for us."

3. Jesus' death provided reconciliation with God.

The word reconciliation means to come in a right relationship with. Through the death of Christ Jesus man's relationship with God has changed. He is no longer alienated or separated from God.

2 Corinthians 5:18-19

"And all things are of God, who hath reconciled us to himself by Jesus Christ, and hath given to us the ministry of reconciliation; To wit, that God was in Christ, reconciling the world unto himself, not imputing their trespasses unto them; and hath committed unto us the word of reconciliation."

As Christians, we have been reconciled with God because our trespasses have been imputed to Christ. God has given us a mandate to proclaim this message of reconciliation.

4. Jesus' death provided propitiation for sin.

The word "propitiation" means "to satisfy." The wrath of God has been satisfied. The death of Christ propitiated God, and allows man to come into a right relationship with God through placing his faith in Christ Jesus as Lord and Savior. Through the death of the Son of God, the Father is satisfied. God's wrath is placed on mankind because of sin. Propitiation for sin is only through the blood of Christ Jesus.

1 John 2:2

"And he is the propitiation for our sins: and not for ours only, but also for the sins of the whole world."

Romans 3:25

"Whom God hath set forth to be a propitiation through faith in his blood, to declare his righ-

teousness for the remission of sins that are past, through the forbearance of God."

5. Jesus' death provided justification.

The word "justification" means "to show righteous." Through the death of Christ Jesus, God declares the believer to be righteous. Justification is a legal term. It tells us that God, who is the universal judge, has in His court declared man not guilty. This verdict is because Christ Jesus took the penalty of man's sin upon Himself when He died.

Romans 5:9

"Much more then, being now justified by his blood, we shall be saved from wrath through him."

Romans 8:33

"Who shall lay any thing to the charge of God's elect? It is God that justifieth."

6. Jesus' death provided adoption.

The word "adoption" means that Jesus has made us His children. As a child of God we are adopted into God's family. This family is called the church. The Holy Spirit allows us to enjoy all the benefits of this new family. Through adoption we are set free from sin and Satan. Through adoption we are blessed with all the spiritual blessings that Jesus our Lord desires to give us.

Galatians 4:1-5

"Now I say, That the heir, as long as he is a child, differeth nothing from a servant, though he be lord of all; But is under tutors and governors until the time appointed of the father. Even so we, when we were children, were in bondage under the elements of the world: But when the fullness of the time was come, God sent forth his Son, made of a woman, made under the law, To redeem them that were under the law, that we might receive the adoption of sons."

Romans 8:15-17

"For ye have not received the spirit of bondage again to fear; but ye have received the Spirit of adoption, whereby we cry, Abba, Father. The Spirit itself beareth witness with our spirit, that we are the children of God: And if children, then heirs; heirs of God, and joint-heirs with Christ; if so be that we suffer with him, that we may be also glorified together."

Adoption therefore sets us free from slavery. We are no longer under Satan's bondage. Adoption qualifies us to be God's children. We become heirs of God, that is, we are guaranteed our eternal salvation.

We are in a relationship with our heavenly Father that allows us to cry out Abba Father. The word "Abba" means "Daddy." It reflects the personal sonship relationship we have with our Father.

7. Jesus' death provided sanctification.

The word "sanctification" means "to be set apart." We have been set apart to be holy vessels. We have been set apart from this ungodly world. We have been set apart as a member of God's family.

The words sanctification, holiness, and saints all come from the same root. The very moment someone believes in Christ Jesus as Savior that person becomes sanctified. Before God the Father we are seen as holy and as saints.

1 Corinthians 6:11

"And such were some of you: but ye are washed, but ye are sanctified, but ye are justified in the name of the Lord Jesus, and by the Spirit of our God."

As Christians, we are washed by the blood of Jesus. We are justified in that we have been made right with God. Our Father in heaven no longer sees our sinful nature. He sees us holy and without blame in Christ Jesus.

Ephesians 1:3-4

"Blessed be the God and Father of our Lord Jesus Christ, who hath blessed us with all spiritual blessings in heavenly places in Christ: According as he hath chosen us in him before the foundation of the world, that we should be holy and without blame before him in love."

As God's children, we should be holy or separated from this world. God has called us to be holy. The Holy Spirit will not work through unholiness.

1 Thessalonians 4:3, 7

"For this is the will of God, even your sanctification, that ye should abstain from fornication. For God hath not called us unto uncleanness, but unto holiness."

Therefore, from a practical perspective, believers are sanctified. That is why we are called saints. At times, however, some believers do not act as saints. Sometimes believers act in the flesh. They are not sensitive to the leading of the Holy Spirit in their lives because of sin. As saints, we should strive to be growing in sanctification. Positionally, that is the way God sees us in relationship to salvation, we are holy and without blame before Him. But practically, we have to be daily growing in sanctification. We must confess our sins and short comings moment by moment. We must have a mind and determination to live right before God and to obey His Word.

2 Corinthians 7:1

"Having therefore these promises, dearly beloved, let us cleanse ourselves from all filthiness of the flesh and spirit, perfecting holiness in the fear of God."

Leviticus 20:7

"Sanctify yourselves therefore, and be ye holy: for I am the Lord your God."

1 Peter 1:15-16

"But as he which hath called you is holy, so be ye holy in all manner of conversation; Because it is written, Be ye holy; for I am holy."

REVIEW

How did sin come upon mankind?

Sin came upon mankind through Adam's disobedience.

How did Jesus take the penalty of our sin upon Himself?

Jesus took the penalty of our sin upon Himself by going to the cross and being crucified for us.

What is the meaning of the word "redemption"?

The word redemption means to pay a price for something; to purchase out of a market; to loose or set free.

What is the meaning of the word "reconciliation"?

The word reconciliation means to come in a right relationship with.

What is the meaning of the word "propitiation"?

The word propitiation means to satisfy. Propitiation for sin is only through the blood of Christ Jesus.

What is the meaning of the word "justification"?

The word justification means to show righteousness.

What is the meaning of the word "adoption"?

The word adoption refers to the fact that Jesus has made us His children through adoption.

What is the meaning of the word "sanctification"?

The word sanctification means to be set apart. God has set us apart from this world to Himself.

Positionally, how does God see believers?

Positionally, God sees believers holy and without blame. This is possible only because of sanctification which Jesus provided on the cross through His blood.

What is the meaning of the word "Abba"?

The word Abba means Daddy. It reflects our personal relationship with our heavenly Father.

C. The Conditions for Salvation

Salvation is dependent solely on faith in Jesus Christ. No other name can be called upon except our Lord Christ Jesus.

Acts 4:10-12

> *"Be it known unto you all, and to all the people of Israel, that by the name of Jesus Christ of Nazareth, whom ye crucified, whom God raised from the dead, even by him doth this man stand here before you whole. This is the stone which was set at nought of you builders,*

> *which is become the head of the corner. Neither is there salvation in any other: for there is none other name under heaven given among men, whereby we must be saved."*

1. God's Love

God's love is shown to us in many ways, but most significantly, God's love is shown in His death for us on the cross. It was on the cross that God provided the way for us to come to Him.

> *John 3:16*
>
> *"For God so loved the world, that he gave his only begotten Son, that whosoever believeth in him should not perish, but have everlasting life."*

2. Man's Condition

God says that all men are in the same condition. All men have sinned and do not measure up to God's standards.

> *Romans 3:23*
>
> *"For all have sinned, and come short of the glory of God."*

3. God's Judgment

The result of our sin has brought the judgment of God upon us and it is clearly stated "death." Death simply and finally means separation. Man is separated from God because of his sin.

Romans 6:23

> "For the wages of sin is death; but the gift of God is eternal life through Jesus Christ our Lord."

4. God's Promise

The greatest love story told is the story of God sending His Son to die for those who have sinned against Him and are unable to save themselves. The question that people ask when they hear that God is willing to forgive their sin and save them is "What must I do?"

Romans 5:8

> "But God commendeth his love toward us, in that, while we were yet sinners, Christ died for us."

5. Man's Response

The unsaved person must simply believe that Christ died for him and then ask Jesus to be his Savior.

Romans 10:9-10

> "That if thou shalt confess with thy mouth the Lord Jesus, and shalt believe in thine heart that God hath raised him from the dead, thou shalt be saved. For with the heart man believeth unto righteousness; and with the mouth confession is made unto salvation."

6. God's Invitation

God invites us to call upon the name of the Lord in order to be saved.

Romans 10:13

"For whosoever shall call upon the name of the Lord shall be saved."

REVIEW

How does God demonstrate His love towards us?

God demonstrated His love for us by sending His Son Christ Jesus to die for our sin. Because of this we have eternal life.

According to Romans 3:23 what is man's condition before God?

All men have sinned and do not measure up to God's standards.

What is the result of our sin?

Sin has bought separation from God. This is referred to as "death."

How should man respond to God's provision for eternal life?

Man should simply believe that Christ died for him and then ask Jesus to be his Savior.

D. The Eternal Security of the Believer

This simply means that the believer can never lose his salvation by sinning, ceasing to believe, or in any other way. This eternal security of the believer is conditioned entirely upon what God does when He saves a soul.

1. Jesus saves believers to the uttermost.

This means that salvation is both complete and eternal.

Hebrews 7:25

> "Wherefore he is able also to save them to the uttermost that come unto God by him, seeing he ever liveth to make intercession for them."

2. Jesus promised that believers should never perish.

Jesus promised us that no one shall ever snatch us out of His hand.

John 10:28-29

> "And I give unto them eternal life; and they shall never perish, neither shall any man pluck them out of my hand. My Father, which gave them me, is greater than all; and no man is able to pluck them out of my Father's hand."

3. Jesus intends to present us faultless before Himself.

Our Lord Jesus will present us faultless because He will keep us from stumbling.

Jude 1:24

"Now unto him that is able to keep you from falling, and to present you faultless before the presence of his glory with exceeding joy."

4. Jesus ever lives to make intercession to keep us saved.

Jesus is our eternal High Priest. He is making intercession for us. Because He intercedes we are kept for all eternity.

1 Peter 1:5

"Who are kept by the power of God through faith unto salvation ready to be revealed in the last time."

5. His Spirit has placed us into the body of Christ.

1 Corinthians 12:13

"For by one Spirit are we all baptized into one body, whether we be Jews or Gentiles, whether we be bond or free; and have been all made to drink into one Spirit."

6. His Spirit has sealed us which is the guarantee of our inheritance.

The sealing of the Holy Spirit takes place at the very moment of salvation. This sealing is permanent. It guarantees our place in heaven.

Ephesians 1:13-14

"In whom ye also trusted, after that ye heard the word of truth, the Gospel of your salvation: in whom also after that ye believed, ye were sealed with that Holy Spirit of promise, Which is the earnest of our inheritance until the redemption of the purchased possession, unto the praise of his glory."

7. His Word guarantees us that nothing shall separate us from the love of Christ.

Romans 8:38-39

"For I am persuaded, that neither death, nor life, nor angels, nor principalities, nor powers, nor things present, nor things to come, Nor height, nor depth, nor any other creature, shall be able to separate us from the love of God, which is in Christ Jesus our Lord."

Eternal security is conditioned entirely upon the grace and work of our heavenly Father. We cannot work for this security. It is all possible because of the cleansing of our sins by the blood of our Lord Christ Jesus. We who are saved are in Christ. We become children of our eternal Father. We have a new identity, a new creation.

REVIEW

How does Jesus save us to the uttermost?

Jesus saves us for all eternity through His shed blood and His ministry as intercessor.

What does it mean to be eternally secure?

It means that the believer can never lose his salvation by sinning, ceasing to believe, or in any other way.

Even though we are eternally secure, how does God expect us to live?

God wants us to live holy and sanctified lives.

Why is it that no one is able to snatch us out of our Father's hand.

No one is able to snatch us out of our Father's hand because our Father is greater than all and has purposed to keep us to Himself.

Where has the Spirit placed believers?

The Spirit has placed believers in the Body of Christ.

Chapter 7

ESCHATOLOGY

Eschatology is the study of the end times—the final days of human history. This period started at the time of the establishment of the church. As we study what the Bible has to say about the end times, we will consider eleven topics. They are as follows:

- The Church Age
- The Rapture of the Church
- The Judgment Seat of Christ
- The Great Tribulation
- The Antichrist
- The Battle of Armageddon
- The Return of Christ
- The Millennium
- The Great White Throne Judgment
- The New Heavens and Earth
- The New Jerusalem

These topics are listed in the order in which they will occur. We must remember that only the Word of God reveals the future. The Bible reveals God's prophetic plan.

A. The Church Age

We are in the time or age of the church. The word "church" means "to call out for a purpose." This church age started on the day of Pentecost, a Jewish feast, which was fifty days after the crucifixion of our Lord Jesus Christ. We read about this event in the book of Acts.

> *Acts 2:1-4*
>
> *"And when the day of Pentecost was fully come, they were all with one accord in one place. And suddenly there came a sound from heaven as of a rushing mighty wind, and it filled all the house where they were sitting. And there appeared unto them cloven tongues like as of fire, and it sat upon each of them. And they were all filled with the Holy Ghost, and began to speak with other tongues, as the Spirit gave them utterance."*

What the disciples experienced was the baptism of the Holy Spirit. This was the very beginning of the church. Our Lord Jesus said that when this baptism takes place, the church will receive power to be witnesses. Our Lord commissioned or ordered the church to share the Gospel message all over the world.

> *Matthew 28:18-20*
>
> *"And Jesus came and spake unto them, saying, All power is given unto me in heaven and in earth. Go ye therefore, and teach all nations, baptizing them in the name of the Father, and of the Son, and of the Holy Ghost: Teaching*

> *them to observe all things whatsoever I have commanded you: and, lo, I am with you alway, even unto the end of the world. Amen."*

The message we have to share in this age is called the Gospel. The word gospel means good news. It is the good news that Jesus Christ came and died for our sins.

<u>Romans 3:23</u>

> *"For all have sinned, and come short of the glory of God."*

What this means is that the sin of Adam brought the consequence of eternal condemnation upon men. Man is no longer able to enter God's heaven. Sin has caused man to fall short of the glory of God.

<u>Romans 6:23</u>

> *"For the wages of sin is death; but the gift of God is eternal life through Jesus Christ our Lord."*

This verse tells us that the wages or penalty of sin is death. This means that the unbeliever is eternally condemned to hell because of sin. God, however, has given us a free gift. This gift is eternal life. It is dependent only upon what our Lord Jesus accomplished through His death, burial, and resurrection. Eternal life cannot be earned since it is a gift. It has to be received by faith.

Romans 10:9-10

"That if thou shalt confess with thy mouth the Lord Jesus, and shalt believe in thine heart that God hath raised him from the dead, thou shalt be saved. For with the heart man believeth unto righteousness; and with the mouth confession is made unto salvation."

Salvation has to be received by faith. The unbeliever must accept the Lord Jesus as his Savior. After seeing his sinful and fallen condition, the unbeliever has to accept the fact that Jesus died for his sins and that God has raised Jesus from the grave.

John 3:16

"For God so loved the world, that he gave his only begotten Son, that whosoever believeth in him should not perish, but have everlasting life."

This verse tells us that salvation is by faith. It is available to everyone. With salvation we receive everlasting life.

1 Corinthians 15:3-4

"For I delivered unto you first of all that which I also received, how that Christ died for our sins according to the scriptures; And that he was buried, and that he rose again the third day according to the scriptures."

The Gospel message should never be distorted. Satan is always trying to distort or change the Gospel message.

He knows that men can be saved only through the Gospel message.

The church has the commission or command to go throughout this world and share the Gospel message. The ultimate or main purpose of the church is to glorify Christ Jesus. Even in the sharing of the Gospel the main purpose is that Christ may be glorified through the saving of souls.

> *Ephesians 3:21*
>
> *"Unto him be glory in the church by Christ Jesus throughout all ages, world without end. Amen."*

REVIEW

What word is often used to mean end times events.

The word is eschatology.

What is the meaning of the word "church"?

The word church means "that which has been called out for a purpose."

When did the church began?

The church began at Pentecost, a Jewish feast that took place fifty days after the crucifixion of our Lord Jesus Christ.

What actually took place on the day of Pentecost?

The Holy Spirit came upon the disciples and others who were praying and baptized and empowered them.

What is the primary purpose of the empowering of the Holy Spirit?

The primary purpose is to glorify Christ through the saving of souls by the proclamation of the Gospel message.

What is the meaning of the word "gospel"?

The word gospel means good news.

What are the fundamentals of the Gospel message?

The fundamentals of the Gospel message is the fact that Jesus came and died for our sins, was buried and rose again the third day.

How must salvation be received?

Salvation must be received by faith in what Jesus did for us on the Cross.

What is the primary purpose of the church?

The primary purpose of the church is to glorify Christ Jesus our Lord.

B. The Rapture of the Church

The next future prophecy in Scripture that will be fulfilled is the Rapture of the church. The word rapture means to be caught up or to take out. The Rapture will bring an end to the church age. At the Rapture our Lord Jesus will call the entire church to heaven. All believers will, at a moment, leave this earth and go to heaven.

> *1 Thessalonians 4:17*
>
> *"Then we which are alive and remain shall be caught up together with them in the clouds, to meet the Lord in the air: and so shall we ever be with the Lord."*

1. The Transformation

When the Rapture takes place, a transformation will occur. This transformation will cause our body to change from this lowly one to a glorious body. This body will be our heavenly body.

> *Philippians 3:20-21*
>
> *"For our conversation is in heaven; from whence also we look for the Savior, the Lord Jesus Christ: Who shall change our vile body, that it may be fashioned like unto his glorious body, according to the working whereby he is able even to subdue all things unto himself."*

2. The Event

The Bible describes the suddenness of the Rapture.

Matthew 24:40-42

> "Then shall two be in the field; the one shall be taken, and the other left. Two women shall be grinding at the mill; the one shall be taken, and the other left. Watch therefore: for ye know not what hour your Lord doth come."

3. The Need to be Ready

The Rapture can take place at any moment. Therefore all Christians need to be ready. Being ready means that we have to be doing those things that we are commanded to do. This is why as Christians we should study God's Word and seek not only to know His Word, but to obey God's Word.

Matthew 24:44-46

> "Therefore be ye also ready: for in such an hour as ye think not the Son of man cometh. Who then is a faithful and wise servant, whom his lord hath made ruler over his household, to give them meat in due season? Blessed is that servant, whom his lord when he cometh shall find so doing."

REVIEW

What event will occur that will bring the church age to an end?

The church will end with the Rapture.

What is the meaning of the word rapture?

The word rapture means to be caught up.

When the Rapture takes place what will happen to our bodies?

Our bodies will be changed to a glorious body.

What will be the timing of the Rapture?

The Rapture can take place at any time. It will be very quick.

C. The Judgment Seat of Christ

After the Rapture, all the believers will appear before the judgment seat of our Lord Christ Jesus. This judgment does not deal with whether or not the believer will enter heaven. The believer has the guarantee to enter heaven. This guarantee is based on the fact that, upon accepting our Lord Jesus as our Savior, we are sealed with the Holy Spirit of promise.

> *Ephesians 1:13-14*
>
> "In whom ye also trusted, after that ye heard the word of truth, the Gospel of your salvation: in whom also after that ye believed, ye

> *were sealed with that Holy Spirit of promise, Which is the earnest of our inheritance until the redemption of the purchased possession, unto the praise of his glory."*

1. The Purpose of the Judgment Seat

The main purpose of the judgment of believers is for the receiving of rewards. These rewards are based on our faithfulness to God.

> *2 Corinthians 5:10*
>
> *"For we must all appear before the judgment seat of Christ; that every one may receive the things done in his body, according to that he hath done, whether it be good or bad."*

2. Explanation of the Event

- Its certainty – "We must"
- Its scope – "All"
- Its location – "Before the judgment seat"
- Its judge – "The Lord Jesus Christ"
- Its purpose – "That each one may be recompensed"
- Basis of the Rewards – "According to what he has done"

3. Evaluation at the Event - 1 Corinthians 3:10-15

   a. The Foundation

   1 Corinthians 3:11

   "For other foundation can no man lay than that is laid, which is Jesus Christ."

   b. The Construction

The Bible describes two types of construction materials, that is, two types of works. There are works which are perishable and works which are nonperishable.

   1 Corinthians 3:12

   "Now if any man build upon this foundation gold, silver, precious stones, wood, hay, stubble."

Works which are perishable are works which may be the result of self. These works do not give glory to God. Works which are nonperishable are those which are the result of the fruit of the Holy Spirit. These works are the results of responding to God's Word. Our Lord Jesus is always glorified through these. Therefore, they bear fruit that last for all eternity.

   4. The Inspection

The fire itself will test the quality of each man's work. This tells us that we have to value our time. We have to be diligent in serving God. The life we live should bear fruit for eternity.

1 Corinthians 3:13

"Every man's work shall be made manifest: for the day shall declare it, because it shall be revealed by fire; and the fire shall try every man's work of what sort it is."

5. The Decision

Jesus Christ, our Righteous Judge, will examine our work based on quality not quantity. This examination will determine what we will lose or what reward we will gain.

1 Corinthians 3:14-15

"If any man's work abide which he hath built thereupon, he shall receive a reward. If any man's work shall be burned, he shall suffer loss: but he himself shall be saved; yet so as by fire."

6. The Reward

1 Corinthians 9:25

"And every man that striveth for the mastery is temperate in all things. Now they do it to obtain a corruptible crown; but we an incorruptible."

The reward mentioned above is an imperishable crown. The Word of God tells us that there are different types of crowns.

a. The Crown of Rejoicing

1 Thessalonians 2:19

"For what is our hope, or joy, or crown of rejoicing? Are not even ye in the presence of our Lord Jesus Christ at his coming?"

b. The Crown of Righteousness

2 Timothy 4:8

"Henceforth there is laid up for me a crown of righteousness, which the Lord, the righteous judge, shall give me at that day: and not to me only, but unto all them also that love his appearing."

God wants us to live righteously. Live each day expecting Christ's imminent return. Our Lord Jesus can come at any moment. His coming is also certain. Therefore, let us live holy and righteous lives.

c. The Crown of Life

The crown of life refers to those who endure suffering for Christ's name. These are the ones who put being faithful to Christ more important than life.

James 1:12

"Blessed is the man that endureth temptation: for when he is tried, he shall receive the crown of life, which the Lord hath promised to them that love him."

Revelation 2:10

"Fear none of those things which thou shalt suffer: behold, the devil shall cast some of you into prison, that ye may be tried; and ye shall have tribulation ten days: be thou faithful unto death, and I will give thee a crown of life."

d. The Crown of Glory

This promise is made to the under-shepherds of the flock. They are the pastors and church leaders who are called to be servants to the congregation or assembly of Christians.

1 Peter 5:2-4

"Feed the flock of God which is among you, taking the oversight thereof, not by constraint, but willingly; not for filthy lucre, but of a ready mind; neither as being lords over God's heritage, but being examples to the flock. And when the chief Shepherd shall appear, ye shall receive a crown of glory that fadeth not away."

7. The Loss of Rewards

At this judgment seat, those works which are not glorifying to God will be burned up, but the believer will be saved. The child of God will never lose his salvation. This promise or guarantee should not cause the believer to live carelessly. It should produce a sense of thankfulness and commitment.

1 Corinthians 3:15

"*If any man's work shall be burned, he shall suffer loss: but he himself shall be saved; yet so as by fire.*"

REVIEW

When will the judgment of believers occur?

The judgment will occur after the Rapture.

What is the purpose of this judgment?

The main purpose is for believers to receive rewards.

What is the basis of the reward?

The reward is based on what the believer has done.

Who will be the judge?

The judge will be our Lord Christ Jesus.

Who is the foundation of our works?

The foundation is our Lord Christ Jesus.

What are the two possible types of works?

The two possible works are works which are perishable and works which are nonperishable

How will the works of the believer be tested?

The works of the believer will be tested by fire.

How will our Lord Christ Jesus make His decision?

Our Lord will examine our works on quality, not quantity.

In the Bible what other word is used for reward?

Another word for reward is crown.

What are the different kinds of crowns?

The different kinds of crowns are:

- Crown of Rejoicing
- Crown of Righteousness
- Crown of Life
- Crown of Glory

D. The Great Tribulation

The Great Tribulation will take place after the Rapture. It will last for a period of seven years.

> <u>Revelation 11:2-3</u>
>
> *"But the court which is without the temple leave out, and measure it not; for it is given unto the Gentiles: and the holy city shall they tread under foot forty and two months. And I will give power unto my two witnesses, and*

they shall prophesy a thousand two hundred and threescore days, clothed in sackcloth."

This time period mentioned in the above verse is one-half of the total period of the Tribulation. It is a period of three and a half years. The Great Tribulation is also called the "time of Jacob's trouble." It is called "Jacob's trouble" because Jeremiah used that term when he prophesied about this time. "Jacob" refers to the nation of Israel.

<u>*Jeremiah 30:7*</u>

"Alas! for that day is great, so that none is like it: it is even the time of Jacob's trouble; but he shall be saved out of it."

Therefore, during the Great Tribulation, God no longer will be working with the church but with Israel as a nation. During the church age there are neither Jews nor Gentiles. However, after the Rapture, God will deal with Israel.

In the book of Daniel, we read about the 70th week of Daniel.

<u>*Daniel 9:24*</u>

"Seventy weeks are determined upon thy people and upon thy holy city, to finish the transgression, and to make an end of sins, and to make reconciliation for iniquity, and to bring in everlasting righteousness, and to seal up the vision and prophecy, and to anoint the most Holy."

Sixty-nine weeks have already passed. There is still one week to come. This one week to come will begin after the

Rapture. Daniel tells us that there will be seven weeks and then sixty-two weeks. This totals sixty-nine weeks. After the sixty-two weeks, the Messiah shall be cut off. This means that the crucifixion shall take place. It does not mean the Messiah is not on the throne. The Messiah is Lord and is fulfilling His divine purpose through His church.

> *Daniel 9:25-26*
>
> *"Know therefore and understand, that from the going forth of the commandment to restore and to build Jerusalem unto the Messiah the Prince shall be seven weeks, and threescore and two weeks: the street shall be built again, and the wall, even in troublous times. And after threescore and two weeks shall Messiah be cut off, but not for himself: and the people of the prince that shall come shall destroy the city and the sanctuary; and the end thereof shall be with a flood, and unto the end of the war desolations are determined."*

Then Daniel tells us that, in the future, Satan will confirm a covenant with Israel for one week. Remember that one week equals to seven years.

Also in the middle of the week the covenant shall be broken. This is why in Revelation 11:2-3 we read about a three and one-half year time period. This is the middle of the Tribulation when Satan turns against Israel. It is also referred to as the abomination of desolation.

> *Daniel 9:27*
>
> *"And he shall confirm the covenant with many for one week: and in the midst of the week he*

shall cause the sacrifice and the oblation to cease, and for the overspreading of abominations he shall make it desolate, even until the consummation, and that determined shall be poured upon the desolate."

During the Great Tribulation, the ministry of the Holy Spirit will not be as it is during this time of the church. The church will not be here. The Rapture would have taken place. During the Great Tribulation, Satan will deceive Israel into worshipping him as the Christ. He will make a covenant or agreement with Israel. In the middle of the Great Tribulation, Satan will break his agreement and turn against Israel. This is what is referred to as "Jacob's trouble."

REVIEW

When will the Great Tribulation begin?

The Great Tribulation will begin immediately after the Rapture.

How long will be the Great Tribulation period?

The Great Tribulation will last for seven years.

How did Jeremiah refer to the Great Tribulation?

Jeremiah referred to the Great Tribulation as "Jacob's trouble."

How did Daniel refer to the Great Tribulation?

Daniel referred to the Great Tribulation as the 70th week.

What event is called the abomination of desolation?

The middle of the seven-year period when Satan kills God's prophets is called the abomination of desolation. After this he turns his wrath on Israel.

E. The Antichrist

The Antichrist is of the seed of Satan. In Genesis we read about the seed of the woman who is Christ and the seed of the serpent who is the Antichrist.

> *Genesis 3:15*
>
> *"And I will put enmity between thee and the woman, and between thy seed and her seed; it shall bruise thy head, and thou shalt bruise his heel."*

1. The Antichrist is a man.

The Bible teaches that the Antichrist is a man. He is not a system. He is a man who will rule in Jerusalem.

> *Revelation 13:18*
>
> *"Here is wisdom. Let him that hath understanding count the number of the beast: for it is the number of a man; and his number is six hundred threescore and six."*

2. The Antichrist will be a Jew.

The Jewish nation will not accept a Gentile as their Messiah. The Bible tells us that the Antichrist will make a covenant with Israel for one week. This one week is the seven years of the Tribulation. Israel will make this covenant only with a Jew.

> *Daniel 9:27a*
>
> *"And he shall confirm the covenant with many for one week...."*

3. The Antichrist will be a commercial genius.

The word teaches that no one will be able to buy or sell without his seal.

> *Revelation 13:17*
>
> *"And that no man might buy or sell, save he that had the mark, or the name of the beast, or the number of his name."*

4. The Antichrist will be a military genius.

> *Revelation 13:4*
>
> *"And they worshipped the dragon which gave power unto the beast: and they worshipped the beast, saying, Who is like unto the beast? Who is able to make war with him?"*

5. The Antichrist will be a religious genius.

   Revelation 13:8

   "And all that dwell upon the earth shall worship him, whose names are not written in the Book of Life of the Lamb slain from the foundation of the world."

6. The Antichrist will be a financial genius.

   Daniel 11:43

   "But he shall have power over the treasures of gold and of silver, and over all the precious things of Egypt: and the Libyans and the Ethiopians shall be at his steps."

7. The Titles of the Antichrist

   a. The Antichrist is called "man of sin."

   2 Thessalonians 2:3

   "Let no man deceive you by any means: for that day shall not come, except there come a falling away first, and that man of sin be revealed, the son of perdition."

   b. The Antichrist is called the son of perdition.

   2 Thessalonians 2:3b

   "...and that man of sin be revealed, the son of perdition."

c. The Antichrist is called the lawless one.

   2 Thessalonians 2:8

   "And then shall that Wicked be revealed, whom the Lord shall consume with the spirit of his mouth, and shall destroy with the brightness of his coming."

   d. His title is "The Antichrist."

   1 John 2:18

   "Little children, it is the last time: and as ye have heard that antichrist shall come, even now are there many antichrists; whereby we know that it is the last time."

REVIEW

Who is the Antichrist?

   The Antichrist is of the seed of Satan.

What is the nature of the Antichrist?

   The Antichrist is a man.

During the Great Tribulation how will the Jewish nation respond to the Antichrist?

   During the first three and one-half years of the Tribulation, the Jews will be deceived into accepting the Antichrist as their Messiah.

In scriptural terms what does one week represent in end-time prophecy?

One week represents a period of seven years.

What are the characteristics of the Antichrist?

The Antichrist's characteristics are as follows:

- He will be a commercial genius.
- He will be a military genius.
- He will be a religious genius.
- He will be a financial genius.

These characteristics will manifest themselves during the Tribulation period.

What are the titles of the Antichrist?

The titles of the Antichrist are as follows:

- Man of sin
- Son of perdition
- Lawless one
- The Antichrist

How do we know that the Antichrist as a man will have to be a Jew?

We know that the Antichrist will have to be a Jew because the Jews will not accept a Gentile as their Messiah.

F. The Battle of Armageddon

The battle of Armageddon will take place at the end of the Great Tribulation. Let us consider the following:

1. Where will this battle take place?

The place of this battle is in the plain of Esdraelon. This is the plain where Saul and Jonathan were killed. It is the valley of Jezreel.

> *1 Samuel 31:7*
>
> *"And when the men of Israel that were on the other side of the valley, and they that were on the other side Jordan, saw that the men of Israel fled, and that Saul and his sons were dead, they forsook the cities, and fled; and the Philistines came and dwelt in them."*

2. When will the battle of Armageddon take place?

The battle of Armageddon will take place at the end of the Great Tribulation. It will be brought to an end with the return of our Lord Christ Jesus.

3. Who will be involved in this battle?

This will be a battle in which Satan will come against Christ.

> *Revelation 19:19*
>
> *"And I saw the beast, and the kings of the earth, and their armies, gathered together to*

> *make war against him that sat on the horse, and against his army."*

Satan's army will comprise of the following:

- The kings of the earth
- The armies of the earth

The person on the horse is Christ Jesus. His army will be His holy Angels.

4. How will the battle of Armageddon end?

This battle will end in the complete destruction of the Antichrist's army. Both the Antichrist and the false prophet will be cast into hell. The false prophet will be the one who will deceive many to take the mark of the beast and to worship the beast. During the Tribulation, the mark of the beast will be given to all those who accept Satan as their Lord. Our Lord Jesus who is Lord of lords and King of kings will conquer Satan and cast all the evil spirits and false prophet into the lake of fire.

Revelation 19:20

> *"And the beast was taken, and with him the false prophet that wrought miracles before him, with which he deceived them that had received the mark of the beast, and them that worshipped his image. These both were cast alive into a lake of fire burning with brimstone."*

REVIEW

When will the battle of Armageddon take place?

It will take place at the end of the Great Tribulation.

How will the battle end?

The battle will end with Satan and the false prophet being cast into hell.

Who will be involved in the battle of Armageddon?

Satan and the kings of the earth, and their armies will be in battle against Christ Jesus and His army of angels.

Where will the battle of Armageddon take place?

The battle of Armageddon will take place in the Plain of Esdraelon.

G. The Return of Christ

The Second Advent or coming of the Lord Christ Jesus will take place at the end of the Tribulation. Jesus will be coming to conquer and to establish. He will conquer Satan and will establish His one-thousand-year kingdom on earth.

1. The Second Advent is promised.

   Acts 1:9-11

   > "And when he had spoken these things, while they beheld, he was taken up; and a cloud received him out of their sight. And while they

looked steadfastly toward heaven as he went up, behold, two men stood by them in white apparel; Which also said, Ye men of Galilee, why stand ye gazing up into heaven? This same Jesus, which is taken up from you into heaven, shall so come in like manner as ye have seen him go into heaven."

2. At His Second Coming, Jesus will once again deal with Israel as a nation.

   Luke 21:20-24

   "And when ye shall see Jerusalem compassed with armies, then know that the desolation thereof is nigh. Then let them which are in Judea flee to the mountains; and let them which are in the midst of it depart out; and let not them that are in the countries enter thereinto. For these be the days of vengeance, that all things which are written may be fulfilled. But woe unto them that are with child, and to them that give suck, in those days! for there shall be great distress in the land, and wrath upon this people. And they shall fall by the edge of the sword, and shall be led away captive into all nations: and Jerusalem shall be trodden down of the Gentiles, until the times of the Gentiles be fulfilled."

3. Jesus' return will be personal.

   Acts 1:11

   "Which also said, Ye men of Galilee, why stand ye gazing up into heaven? This same Jesus, which is taken up from you into heaven, shall so come in like manner as ye have seen him go into heaven."

4. Jesus coming will be visible.

   Zechariah 12:10-11

   "And I will pour upon the house of David, and upon the inhabitants of Jerusalem, the spirit of grace and of supplications: and they shall look upon me whom they have pierced, and they shall mourn for him, as one mourneth for his only son, and shall be in bitterness for him, as one that is in bitterness for his firstborn. In that day shall there be a great mourning in Jerusalem, as the mourning of Hadadrimmon in the valley of Megiddon."

   Revelation 1:7

   "Behold, he cometh with clouds; and every eye shall see him, and they also which pierced him: and all kindreds of the earth shall wail because of him. Even so, Amen."

5. Jesus' return to earth will be with his saints.

It is interesting that we will be involved in the Second Advent of the Lord Christ Jesus.

Jude 1:14

"And Enoch also, the seventh from Adam, prophesied of these, saying, Behold, the Lord cometh with ten thousands of his saints."

6. When Jesus returns his name will be called "The Word of God."

The title "The Word of God" is telling us that his coming is the fulfillment of the Word of God.

Revelation 19:13

"And he was clothed with a vesture dipped in blood: and his name is called The Word of God."

7. He will come as Judge.

Revelation 19:11

"And I saw heaven opened, and behold a white horse; and he that sat upon him was called Faithful and True, and in righteousness he doth judge and make war."

8. Jesus will return to conquer.

   Revelation 19:15

   "And out of his mouth goeth a sharp sword, that with it he should smite the nations: and he shall rule them with a rod of iron: and he treadeth the winepress of the fierceness and wrath of Almighty God."

9. When Jesus returns the world will know that he is both King and Lord.

   Revelation 19:16

   "And he hath on his vesture and on his thigh a name written, KING OF KINGS, AND LORD OF LORDS."

10. At his Second Advent Jesus will bind Satan for a thousand years.

    Revelation 20:2

    "And he laid hold on the dragon, that old serpent, which is the Devil, and Satan, and bound him a thousand years."

11. Christ will judge the world.

This judgment will occur at the Second Coming of our Lord Christ Jesus. It is called the "sheep-goat judgment." Our Lord will be the judge. During this event both Jews and Gentiles will be judged. The judgment will be based on whether the person is saved or lost. The result will be that the saved will enter the Kingdom Age while the lost will be placed in eternal hell fire. Therefore, there will be a separating of the saved from the lost. The saved are referred to as the sheep while the unsaved are referred to as goats. Thus, the term sheep-goat judgment refers to the separating of the two.

REVIEW

When will the Second Advent take place?

It will take place at the end of the Great Tribulation.

What is the meaning of the term "Second Advent"?

The term Second Advent means the second time that our Lord Christ Jesus comes to the earth.

What is the primary purpose for our Lord's Second Advent?

The main purpose is to bind Satan so that the Millennial Kingdom can run its course without deception or interference.

What will Jesus' relationship be with Israel at his Second Advent?

At his Second Advent, Jesus will deal with Israel as a nation. The church would have been raptured seven years before his return.

What will be our role at His Second Advent?

At His Second Advent we will come with Him as He conquers.

What is the meaning of the title "The Word of God"?

The title The Word of God means that Jesus' coming will be a fulfillment of Scripture.

For how long will Jesus bind Satan at His Second Coming?

Jesus will bind Satan for one thousand years (a millennium).

When will the sheep-goat judgment occur?

The sheep-goat judgment will occur at the Second Coming of Christ.

Who will be the judge?

Christ Jesus our Lord will be the judge.

Who will be judged?

All those who will be alive at His coming will be judged.

What will be the basis of the judgment?

Judgment will be based on whether the individual is saved or unsaved.

What will happen to those who are saved?

They will enter the Millennial Kingdom.

What will happen to those who are lost?

The lost will be cast into the lake of fire.

According to Matthew Chapter 25, who are the sheep and goats?

The sheep are those who are saved and the goats are those who are lost.

H. The Millennium

The word "Millennium" refers to a future one-thousand-year period. During this time period, Christ will reign as King.

1. Description of the Millennium

The Millennium has been referred to by different terms.

    a. The kingdom of heaven

<u>Matthew 6:10</u>

"Your kingdom come. Your will be done on earth as it is in heaven."

    b. The Millennium is described as "the age to come."

Ephesians 1:20-21

"Which he wrought in Christ, when he raised him from the dead, and set him at his own right hand in the heavenly places, Far above all principality, and power, and might, and dominion, and every name that is named, not only in this world, but also in that which is to come."

c. The Millennium is described as "the day of the Lord."

Joel 2:11

"And the Lord shall utter his voice before his army: for his camp is very great: for he is strong that executeth his word: for the day of the Lord is great and very terrible; and who can abide it?"

d. The Millennium is described as "in that day."

Isaiah 4:2

"In that day shall the branch of the Lord be beautiful and glorious, and the fruit of the earth shall be excellent and comely for them that are escaped of Israel."

> Note: In the above verse, the term "branch of the lord" means Messiah or Christ Jesus.

e. The Millennium is described as "the restoration of all things."

Acts 3:20-21

"And he shall send Jesus Christ, which before was preached unto you: Whom the heaven must receive until the times of restitution of all things, which God hath spoken by the mouth of all his holy prophets since the world began."

f. The Millennium is described as "the kingdom of God."

Luke 19:11

"And as they heard these things, he added and spake a parable, because he was nigh to Jerusalem, and because they thought that the kingdom of God should immediately appear."

g. The Millennium is described as "the kingdom of Christ."

Revelation 11:15

"And the seventh angel sounded; and there were great voices in heaven, saying, The kingdoms of this world are become the kingdoms of our Lord, and of his Christ; and he shall reign for ever and ever."

h. The Millennium has been described as "the regeneration."

Matthew 19:28

"And Jesus said unto them, Verily I say unto you, That ye which have followed me, in the regeneration when the Son of man shall sit in the throne of his glory, ye also shall sit upon twelve thrones, judging the twelve tribes of Israel."

i. The Millennium has been described as "the times of refreshing."

Acts 3:19

"Repent ye therefore, and be converted, that your sins may be blotted out, when the times of refreshing shall come from the presence of the Lord."

j. The Millennium has been described as "the world to come."

Hebrews 2:5

"For unto the angels hath he not put in subjection the world to come, whereof we speak."

> Note: In this verse we see that the world to come which is the millennial kingdom will be ruled, not by angels, but by our Lord Christ Jesus and we who have been redeemed.

2. Conditions during the Millennium

    a. The Church

During the Millennium we who are redeemed will be judges. Even the angels will be subject to our rule. The saints will judge the world.

> *1 Corinthians 6:2-3*
>
> *"Do ye not know that the saints shall judge the world? and if the world shall be judged by you, are ye unworthy to judge the smallest matters? Know ye not that we shall judge angels? how much more things that pertain to this life?"*
>
> *2 Timothy 2:11-12*
>
> *"It is a faithful saying: For if we be dead with him, we shall also live with him: If we suffer, we shall also reign with him: if we deny him, he also will deny us."*

3. Satan

During the Millennium, Satan will be bound until the end. After the thousand years, Satan will be loose in order to deceive the nations.

> *Revelation 20:1-3*
>
> *"And I saw an angel come down from heaven, having the key of the bottomless pit and a great chain in his hand. And he laid hold*

on the dragon, that old serpent, which is the Devil, and Satan, and bound him a thousand years, And cast him into the bottomless pit, and shut him up, and set a seal upon him, that he should deceive the nations no more, till the thousand years should be fulfilled: and after that he must be loosed a little season."

Revelation 20:7-8

"And when the thousand years are expired, Satan shall be loosed out of his prison, And shall go out to deceive the nations which are in the four quarters of the earth, Gog and Magog, to gather them together to battle: the number of whom is as the sand of the sea."

4. Israel

Israel will become the head of all nations.

Zechariah 8:23

"Thus saith the Lord of hosts; In those days it shall come to pass, that ten men shall take hold out of all languages of the nations, even shall take hold of the skirt of him that is a Jew, saying, We will go with you: for we have heard that God is with you."

> Note: We also see in this verse that during the Millennium the Gentiles will seek the blessings and knowledge of God.

5. The Government

   a. Christ will be the Head.

   Revelation 19:16

   "And he hath on his vesture and on his thigh a name written, KING OF KINGS, AND LORD OF LORDS."

   b. Spiritual Condition

There will be a universal order of Christ. Everyone will know that Jesus is the Christ.

   Hebrews 8:11

   "And they shall not teach every man his neighbor, and every man his brother, saying, Know the Lord: for all shall know me, from the least to the greatest."

   c. Physical Condition

Human life will be lengthened. There will be no death to babes or children. When an unbeliever gets to one hundred years old, if he refuses to accept the Lordship of Christ he will die.

   Isaiah 65:20

   "There shall be no more thence an infant of days, nor an old man that hath not filled his days: for the child shall die an hundred years

old; but the sinner being an hundred years old shall be accursed."

    d. Moral Condition

During the Millennium justice and peace will reign. Sin, however, will exist. However, sin will not be allowed to increase. Christ shall judge the nations.

Isaiah 2:4

"And he shall judge among the nations, and shall rebuke many people: and they shall beat their swords into plowshares, and their spears into pruninghooks: nation shall not lift up sword against nation, neither shall they learn war any more."

    e. The Capital of the World

During the Millennium, the capital of the world will be Jerusalem.

Isaiah 2:1-3

"The word that Isaiah the son of Amoz saw concerning Judah and Jerusalem. And it shall come to pass in the last days, that the mountain of the Lord's house shall be established in the top of the mountains, and shall be exalted above the hills; and all nations shall flow unto it. And many people shall go and say, Come ye, and let us go up to the mountain of the Lord, to the house of the God of Jacob; and he will teach us of his ways, and we will walk in his *paths: for out of Zion shall go forth the law, and the word of the Lord from Jerusalem."*

REVIEW

What is the meaning of the word "Millennium"?

The word Millennium means one thousand years.

What are the descriptions of the Millennium?

The descriptions of the Millennium are as follows:

- The kingdom of heaven
- The age to come
- The day of the Lord
- In that day
- The restoration of all things
- The kingdom of God
- The kingdom of Christ
- The regeneration
- The times of refreshing
- The world to come

Who will rule during the Millennium?

Our Lord Jesus Christ will rule as King and Lord during the Millennium.

What does the term "Branch of the Lord" mean?

Branch of the Lord refers to Messiah or Christ Jesus.

What role will the church play during the Millennium?

During the Millennium we who are the redeemed will rule with our Lord Jesus Christ and be judges.

What will happen to Satan during the Millennium?

During the Millennium, Satan will be bound.

What will happen to Satan after the Millennium?

After the Millennium, Satan will be loose in order to deceive the nations.

What will be the function of the Jews who enter the Millennium?

They will become heads of all nations.

What will be the spiritual condition during the Millennium?

There will be universal order under the leadership of Christ. Everyone will acknowledge Christ as Lord of lords and King of kings.

What will be the physical condition during the Millennium?

During the Millennium, human life will be lengthen. Babies and children will not die. Anyone who lives to be hundred years old and refuses to accept the Lordship of Christ will die.

During the Millennium, what will be the moral condition?

During the Millennium even though sin will exist, justice and peace will reign. Through the judgment of Christ, sin will not be allowed to prevail.

What will be the capital of the world during the Millennium?

Jerusalem will be the capital of the world.

6. After the Millennium

After the Millennium, Satan will be loosed in order to deceive the nations. The nations will reject God and follow Satan. This will prove without any doubt that man even when he is given the opportunity to live righteous before God will become rebellious. Man has no excuse for the judgment due him.

These then are the order of events immediately after the Millennium.

    a. Satan will be released from his prison.

    Revelation 20:7

    "And when the thousand years are expired, Satan shall be loosed out of his prison."

    b Satan will deceive all the nations of the earth to battle against God.

Revelation 20:8

"And shall go out to deceive the nations which are in the four quarters of the earth, Gog and Magog, to gather them together to battle: the number of whom is as the sand of the sea."

> Note: Gog and Magog symbolize the worldwide enemies of Christ.

c. God sends fire from heaven and destroys mankind.

Revelation 20:9

"And they went up on the breadth of the earth, and compassed the camp of the saints about, and the beloved city: and fire came down from God out of heaven, and devoured them."

d. Satan and the false prophet are cast into eternal hell fire.

Revelation 20:10

"And the devil that deceived them was cast into the lake of fire and brimstone, where the beast and the false prophet are, and shall be tormented day and night for ever and ever."

REVIEW

What will happen to Satan immediately after the Millennium?

Satan will be released from his prison immediately after the Millennium.

What will Satan accomplished after his release?

After Satan has been released, he will deceive the world to battle against Christ.

What does Gog and Magog symbolize?

Gog and Magog symbolize the worldwide enemies of Christ.

What will be the final result of this great battle?

God will send fire from heaven to destroy his enemies.

What will be the final destiny of Satan and his false prophet?

The devil and the false prophet will be cast into hell where they will be tormented forever.

I. The Great White Throne Judgment

The great white throne judgment is the final judgment. It will be only for unbelievers. All born-again believers would have been in heaven at this judgment. The unbelieving dead will experience a resurrection then a condemnation.

Revelation 20:11-12a

"And I saw a great white throne, and him that sat on it, from whose face the earth and the heaven fled away; and there was found no place for them. And I saw the dead, small and great, stand before God...."

The dead who experience this resurrection and judgment will be judged according to their work. Since they have rejected Christ Jesus they will be condemned.

Revelation 20:12

"And I saw the dead, small and great, stand before God; and the books were opened: and another book was opened, which is the Book of Life: and the dead were judged out of those things which were written in the books, according to their works."

During this judgment, anyone's name not found written in the Book of Life was eternally condemned.

Revelation 20:15

"And whosoever was not found written in the Book of Life was cast into the lake of fire."
During this judgment all unbelievers will stand before Christ."

Revelation 20:12a

"And I saw the dead, small and great, stand before God..."

> Note: The term "standing before God" means standing before the throne of Christ where he is the judge.

REVIEW

When will the great white throne judgment occur?

It will take place after the Millennium.

Who will be judged at the great white throne judgment?

All unbelievers will be judged at the great white throne judgment.

Who will be the judge?

Our Lord Christ Jesus will be the judge.

What will be the final end of all unbelievers?

All unbelievers will be cast into eternal fire.

What will be the function of the "Book of Life"?

The Book of Life will be used to judge those who will be condemned. If anyone's name is not found written in the Book of Life, he or she will be cast into the lake of fire.

J. The New Heaven and New Earth

After the great white throne judgment, God will establish a new heaven and a new earth. Let us now consider facts about the new heaven and the new earth.

1. The new heaven and the new earth will be renovated by fire.

    2 Peter 3:12

    "Looking for and hasting unto the coming of the day of God, wherein the heavens being on fire shall be dissolved, and the elements shall melt with fervent heat?"

2. In the new heaven and the new earth, there will be no sin, there will be only righteousness. Praise God for his eternal blessings!

    2 Peter 3:13

    "Nevertheless we, according to his promise, look for new heavens and a new earth, wherein dwelleth righteousness."

K. The New Jerusalem

1. The name New Jerusalem signifies the purity and holiness of God.

    Revelation 21:10

    "And he carried me away in the Spirit to a great and high mountain, and showed me that

great city, the holy Jerusalem, descending out of heaven from God."

2. Names of the New Jerusalem

   a. The New Jerusalem is called the Tabernacle of God.

The City received this title because it is where God and all the saints dwell.

Revelation 21:3

"And I heard a great voice out of heaven saying, Behold, the tabernacle of God is with men, and he will dwell with them, and they shall be his people, and God himself shall be with them, and be their God."

   b. A Bride Adorned for her Husband

The New Jerusalem is called so because it is the dwelling place of all the redeemed. Believers who are the redeemed have been purchased by the blood of Christ Jesus. We belong to him.

Revelation 21:2

"And I John saw the holy city, New Jerusalem, coming down from God out of heaven, prepared as a bride adorned for her husband."

c. The Great City

It is called the Great City because it is the capital of the universe.

> *Revelation 21:10*
>
> *"And he carried me away in the Spirit to a great and high mountain, and showed me that great city, the holy Jerusalem, descending out of heaven from God."*

d. The Heavenly Jerusalem

It is called the heavenly Jerusalem symbolizing the holiness and might of God.

e. The Size of the City

The New Jerusalem will be twelve thousand furlongs in length and breath and height. Twelve thousand furlongs is approximately 1,500 miles.

> *Revelation 21:16*
>
> *"And the city lieth foursquare, and the length is as large as the breadth: and he measured the city with the reed, twelve thousand furlongs. The length and the breadth and the height of it are equal."*

f. The Ruler of the New Jerusalem

Our Lord Jesus who is the Lamb of God shall rule the City from the Throne of God.

Revelation 22:3

"And there shall be no more curse: but the throne of God and of the Lamb shall be in it; and his servants shall serve Him."

Hebrews 12:22

"But ye are come unto mount Zion, and unto the city of the living God, the heavenly Jerusalem, and to an innumerable company of angels."

g. My Father's House

It is called "My Father's House" because our Lord Jesus is presently there preparing our dwelling places.

John 14:1-3

"Let not your heart be troubled: ye believe in God, believe also in me. In my Father's house are many mansions: if it were not so, I would have told you. I go to prepare a place for you. And if I go and prepare a place for you, I will come again, and receive you unto myself; that where I am, there ye may be also."

REVIEW

When will the new heaven and New Jerusalem begin?

It will be established after the great white throne judgment.

What will be used in the renovation of the new earth?

The new earth will be renovated by fire.

What are the titles for the New Jerusalem?

The titles of the New Jerusalem are as follows:

- The Tabernacle
- A Bride Adorned for her Husband
- The Great City
- The Heavenly Jerusalem
- My Father's House

What will be the size of the New Jerusalem?

Its length, breadth and height will be approximately 1,500 miles.

Who will dwell in the New Jerusalem?

This City will be developed for all believers. It will be the dwelling place of the saints.

Who will rule in the New Jerusalem?

Its ruler will be our Lord Christ Jesus.

Chapter 8

Christian Living

The Christian

The Christian life is defined by a personal relationship with God through Christ Jesus our Lord. In order for you to experience the Christian life, you must first be a Christian. You can be sure that you are a Christian.

Our Need for a Savior

Whether Jew or Gentile, everyone has a sin problem.

<u>Romans 3:23</u>

"For all have sinned, and come short of the glory of God."

This sin problem started in the Garden of Eden when Adam and Eve disobeyed God. Because every person is a descendant of Adam, this sin has caused us all to fall short of the glory of God. The glory of God, however, rests in the person of Jesus Christ. By His sinless life, our Lord Jesus Christ reveals the holy glory of God. Sin, however, causes us to fall short of the holiness of Christ. We are not able to measure up to the holiness of Christ. Since we have fallen short of the glory of God, we are unable to enter God's heaven because there is no sin in heaven.

The wages of sin, or the penalty of sin, is death. This means both a spiritual and a physical death. There is always a consequence for sin. The consequence of spiritual death is that man is unable to enter heaven. Man is eternally condemned to this sinful state.

Romans 6:23

"For the wages of sin is death; but the gift of God is eternal life through Jesus Christ our Lord."

The good news is that God has given us a gift. This gift is eternal life, which came through our Lord Jesus Christ. Jesus paid the price for the consequence, or wages, of our sin. Without this provision, no one could be saved.

One day, all unsaved people will stand before the judgment of God. This judgment will determine the degree of punishment a person will receive. This judgment is also called "the great white throne judgment".

Romans 2:6

"Who will render to every man according to his deed."

All unsaved people who refuse to accept the Lord Jesus as their personal Savior will experience God's wrath of tribulation and anguish. The word "wrath" means a sudden outburst of anger. This is the anger of God on man because of sin.

Romans 2:8-9

"But unto them that are contentious, and do not obey the truth, but obey unrighteousness, indignation and wrath. Tribulation and anguish, upon every soul of man that doeth evil, of the Jew first, and also of the Gentile."

John 3:36

"He that believeth on the Son hath everlasting life; and he that believeth not the Son shall not see life; but the wrath of God abideth on him."

Through Adam, mankind fell short of the glory of God. Consequently, those people who reject God's gift of eternal life through Christ Jesus will experience God's wrath. Sin leads to both spiritual and physical death. This means that mankind is all-deserving of eternal suffering in hell. This is why we need our Savior, Christ Jesus. Only Jesus, who is the all holy and righteous God, can provide the gift of eternal life. Praise God for Christ Jesus meeting our need!

The Christ

Jesus is God and one with the Father and the Holy Spirit. Together, these three make up the Godhead. The Father, the Son (Jesus Christ), and the Holy Spirit are equal in power and glory; however, the Father is not the Son, the Son is not the Holy Spirit, and the Holy Spirit is not the Father. Even though they are different personalities, they are one God.

<u>Philippians 2:6</u>

"Who, being in the form of God, did not consider it robbery to be equal with God."

<u>1 John 5:7</u>

"For there are three that bear record in heaven, the Father, the Word, and the Holy Ghost: and these three are one."

Note that in this verse, the term "the Word" is referring to our Lord Christ Jesus.

Jesus was conceived by the power of the Holy Spirit and was born of a virgin. Because Jesus was born as a man, He is a descendant of Adam. Jesus had all of the qualities that Adam had before his fall from God's grace except He did not have the sinful nature that came through Adam's fall.

<u>Philippians 2:7</u>

"But made Himself of no reputation, and took upon him the form of a servant, and was made in the likeness of men."

The phrase "made Himself of no reputation" means that Jesus emptied Himself, that is, He willingly refrained from exercising His authority as God and chose to live as a human. Although Jesus emptied Himself in order to live as a man, He was not less than, or became less than, God. Jesus did not give up any of His divine attributes. He is fully man and fully God. This is a mystery, yet we accept it by faith.

Philippians 2:8

"And being found in fashion as a man, he humbled himself and became obedient unto the point of death, even the death of the cross."

This verse tells us how far Jesus went in His humiliation and obedience. Jesus humbled Himself to the point of death on the cross. Jesus' humility revealed His love for mankind. Because of His love, He volunteered Himself to endure the suffering of the cross, the most horrible death of shame that anyone could suffer. Christ became our voluntary substitute and, in so doing, won the victory for us over death.

Through Jesus' humility and obedience, He received again the glory He shared with the Father as sovereign over everything.

Philippians 2:9

"Wherefore God also hath highly exalted him and given him a name which is above every name."

Philippians 2:10-11

"That at the name of Jesus, ever knee should bow, of things in heaven, and things in earth, and things under the earth, and that every tongue should confess that Jesus Christ is Lord, to the glory of God the Father."

Because of Jesus' atonement for man, every person will eventually have to acknowledge His Lordship. All spiritual beings will bow to Christ and openly profess that He is Lord. Even today, whenever men acknowledge the Lordship of Christ, God the Father is glorified.

1 Corinthians 15:3

> *"For I delivered unto you first of all that which I also received, how that Christ died for our sins according to the scriptures."*

Jesus died for our sins. He became man's substitute, that is, He paid the price for our sins. We could not do it ourselves. Our Lord Jesus, who is all-holy and righteous, became the sacrifice for the penalty of our sins.

1 Corinthians 15:4

> *"And that he was buried, and that he rose again the third day according to the scriptures."*

It was necessary that Christ die for our sins. The victory of His death is that He rose from the grave on the third day. His resurrection proves His victory over death. Because of Christ's obedience, we have salvation and a faithful High Priest who is seated at the Father's right hand.

Salvation through Faith

God's desire is that everyone who sees or hears of the Son might believe in Him. It is this belief that brings the salvation that our Lord has provided. It is man's responsibility to accept, by faith, the salvation that Jesus has provided.

John 6:40

> *"And this is the will of him who sent me, that everyone which seeth the Son, and believeth in him, may have everlasting life: and I will raise him up at the last day."*

Man must respond to God by sincere confession of his belief in Christ and his genuine belief that He is the Savior. The confession of the Lordship of Christ presupposes the incarnation, death, and resurrection of Jesus.

<u>Romans 10:9</u>

"That if thou shalt confess with thy mouth the Lord Jesus, and shalt believe in thine heart that God hath raised him from the dead, thou shalt be saved."

A person's belief that Jesus is the Christ must come from the innermost part of her being, or her heart. This sincere belief of the heart must then be followed by confession with the mouth. It is possible that someone can confess that Christ is Lord with their mouth, but not truly believe that He is Lord. Therefore, two things must be evident: genuine belief and confession.

<u>Romans 10:10</u>

"For with the heart man believeth unto righteousness; and with the mouth confession is made unto salvation."

God is willing and ready to accept all sinners.

<u>Romans 10:13</u>

"For whosoever shall call upon the name of the Lord shall be saved."

This verse reveals the abundant blessings of God's grace. Anyone who calls on Him will be saved. God has made this gift of eternal life available to all. However, we have a responsibility to receive God's gift through faith. The Holy Spirit opens our hearts and draws us to Christ, but it is still up to us whether we will accept or refuse God's gift of eternal life.

God chose us to experience this new creation, or new birth. We could not come to Him if He did not first draw us to Himself. It is God's grace that gives us the opportunity to accept Jesus as our Savior.

John 6:44

"No man can come to me, except the Father which hath sent me draw him: and I will raise him up at the last day."

John 6:65

"And he said, Therefore said I unto you, that no man can come unto me, except it were given unto him of my Father."

The Christian Life

Once a person accepts by faith what our Lord Jesus did for mankind on Calvary, he is "born again," or experiences a spiritual rebirth. A Christian is someone who has experienced a spiritual birth through faith in the Lord Jesus Christ and, henceforth, experiences a personal, daily relationship with Christ.

John 3:3

"Jesus answered and said unto him, Verily, verily, I say unto thee, Except a man be born again, he cannot see the kingdom of God."

The New Nature

At the very instant a person accepts Christ Jesus as his Lord and Savior; he becomes a new creation free of the Adamic curse. The Adamic curse, which resulted in the penalty of spiritual death, is now lifted. The believer becomes a new creation and his relationship with God changes forever. He is no longer condemned. From this time forward, God sees the believer as being washed by the blood of Christ, holy and without blame before Him.

2 Corinthians 5:17

"Therefore if any man be in Christ, he is a new creature: old things are passed away; behold, all things are become new."

The New Relationship

A Christian has a new relationship with God—a sonship relationship. The Christian acknowledges God as his "Abba Father." We can freely address God as we would our own father. This supernatural birth is God's will being worked out in the life of the believer and is only possible by the grace of God. Remember that the grace of God means God's favor, or kindness, toward us. God did not ask man to be good to receive His blessing; He blessed man only because He loves him.

John 1:12-13

"But as many as receive him, to them gave he power to become the sons of God, even to them that believe on his name: Which were born, not of blood, nor of the will of the flesh, nor of the will of man, but of God."

Romans 8:14-16

"For as many as are led by the Spirit of God, they are the sons of God. For ye have not received the spirit of bondage again to fear; but ye have received the Spirit of adoption, whereby we cry, 'Abba, Father.' The Spirit itself beareth witness with our spirit, that we are the children of God."

Christians have received Jesus as their Savior. They have made a personal choice to accept Jesus for themselves. They placed their trust in Christ and are in total dependence upon Him and what He has provided for them.

Ephesians 2:8-9

"For by grace are ye saved through faith; and that not of yourselves: it is the gift of God: Not of works, lest any man should boast."

We have done nothing to deserve this gift of a new birth. We are a new creation only because of God's grace. Grace means what God has done for us; not what we have done for God.

The need for salvation is man's greatest need, and salvation is God's greatest gift to man. It is by grace that salvation is made available to us. It is by faith that we receive the gift of salvation. We could not work to earn this gift of salvation. It cannot be attained by self-effort. It is indeed a free gift of God.

REVIEW

Who is Jesus by nature?

Jesus is God and one with the Father and the Holy Spirit.

What does "made Himself of no reputation" mean?

This phrase means that Jesus left His heavenly throne and came to earth in the form of a man.

To what did Jesus humble Himself?

Jesus humbled Himself to the death on the cross.

What does it mean that Jesus became our substitute?

Jesus died in mankind's place. He paid the price for our sin problem.

Why did Jesus die?

Jesus died for our sins so that we could be restored to a right relationship with God.

Because of Christ's obedience, where did God the Father seat Him?

The Father has seated Jesus at His right hand. Thus, Jesus is sovereign over everything.

What does "come short of the glory of God" mean?

To come short of the glory of God means that mankind is not able to measure up to the holiness of Christ.

How many people have sinned?

All men have sinned.

What does the word "wages" mean?

The word "wages" means penalty, price, or consequence.

What is the wages of sin?

The wages of sin is death.

What type of death does an unbeliever experience?

An unbeliever experiences both a spiritual death and a physical death.

What gift did God give mankind?

God gave man the gift of eternal life.

What is God's will for all men?

God's will for men is that all might be saved.

What does Jesus promise to the believer?

Jesus promises Christians that once they are saved, they will never lose their salvation.

How should a person respond to God's gift?

Man should genuinely believe in his heart that Jesus came and died for his sins on Calvary.

What two things does the Bible say must be done in order to be saved?

In order to be saved, a person must confess with his mouth and believe in his heart that Jesus Christ is Lord.

What does the confession "Jesus is Lord" refer to?

This phrase refers to the Lordship that Jesus exercises as the exalted Christ.

What must man understand about Jesus in order for his confession to save him?

Man must understand that God came in the person of Jesus Christ, that He died for our sins, was buried and that He rose on the third day.

What does confession signify?

Confession is the evidence of genuine belief in the heart.

Who is a Christian?

A Christian is someone who has experienced a spiritual birth through his faith in the Lord Jesus Christ.

At what point in the Christian life does a believer become a new creation?

At the very instant that someone accepts Christ Jesus as his Lord and Savior, she becomes a new creation.

When a believer becomes a new creation in Christ, how does it affect her relationship with God?

God sees the Christian as being washed by the blood of Christ Jesus, holy and righteous.

How is the unsaved man drawn to God?

God, by His grace, draws the unsaved man to Himself through the Holy Spirit.

What does "born again" mean?

To be born again means to experience a spiritual rebirth by trusting that Jesus Christ is Lord and Savior.

Where is the kingdom of God?

The kingdom of God is the heavenly place where Jesus sits on the throne as King.

What does it mean to believe in the Lord Jesus Christ as Savior?

Believing that Jesus is the Savior means that we have placed our trust fully in Christ.

What does the word "grace" mean?

Grace means "undeserved or unmerited favor."

When someone accepts Jesus as his Savior, how does this affect his relationship with the heavenly Father?

When a believer accepts Christ as his Savior, he becomes the adopted son of God.

What does the phrase "all things have become new" mean?

The phrase "all things have become new" means that the believer is no longer under the Adamic curse. God recognizes him as His son, as a new creation.

Chapter 9

Prayer

What is prayer?

Prayer is simply talking with God. When we pray, we are communicating with our heavenly Father who loves us. Prayer is the lifeblood of the Christian. The Christian needs prayer in order to live. Our Lord Jesus taught us in Luke 18:1 that we should always pray.

> *Luke 18:1*
>
> *"And he spake a parable unto them to this end, that men ought always to pray, and not to faint."*

While our Lord Jesus lived on earth, He always prayed. By His example, we should likewise live a life of prayer. Even now, our Lord Jesus is praying on our behalf. He is making intercession, or praying on behalf of us to God.

Hebrews 7:25

"Wherefore he is able also to save them to the uttermost that come unto God by him, seeing he ever liveth to make intercession for them."

Intercession means to pray for another person's needs. Christians experience the power of the Holy Spirit in their life through prayer.

Prayer causes us to depend fully upon God. When we pray to God, we make ourselves available to His service, yielding our lives as a living sacrifice. In Romans 12:1, we can clearly see how God wants us to present our lives to Him, to spiritually worship Him.

Romans 12:1

"I beseech you therefore, brethren, by the mercies of God, that ye present your bodies a living sacrifice, holy, acceptable unto God, which is your reasonable service."

God's Word says that yielding our lives is our "reasonable service."

The Elements of Prayer

Although praying is simply talking with our Father, Jesus did teach us several important points about praying, all of which are covered in this section.

Praise

Praise is the most important key to experiencing a powerful prayer life. God has set apart His church to praise

Him. Our Lord Jesus, in teaching us to pray, said that we should hallow God's name, or "set apart" or "glorify" His name. Hallowing God's name means you are lifting up or worshipping God.

Matthew 6:9

"After this manner therefore pray ye: Our Father which art in heaven, Hallowed be thy name."

To hallow God's name is to be in reverence and awe of His holiness. Our God is all-holy. He wants us to enter His presence through praise. Throughout this life and all of eternity, God desires that His children praise Him. What then is praise? Praise is the vocal adoration of God in which we express our love for God. This is why God accepts our praise as glorifying Him.

Praise also reveals the presence of God. As God's people praise Him, the presence of His glory is revealed.

Psalm 50:23a

"Whoso offereth praise glorifieth me."

2 Chronicles 5:13-14

"It came even to pass, as the trumpeters and singers were as one, to make one sound to be heard in praising and thanking the Lord; and when they lifted up their voice with the trumpets and cymbals and instruments of music, and praised the Lord, saying, For he is good; for his mercy endureth for ever: that then the house was filled with a cloud, even the house of the Lord; So that the priests could not stand to minister by

reason of the cloud: for the glory of the Lord had filled the house of God."

This Scripture tells us that God inhabits our praises. Thus, as we praise God, His holiness and presence is felt.

Psalm 22:3

"But thou art holy, O thou that inhabitest the praises of Israel."

We should praise God in the midst of trials. We must praise God as we pray, even when we are faced with many trials. We praise God because He is God. This is referred to as offering up sacrifices of praise.

Hebrews 13:15

"By him therefore let us offer the sacrifice of praise to God continually, that is, the fruit of our lips giving thanks to his name."

We should praise God for His name. All of God's names describe His attributes and character.

Psalm 115:1

"Not unto us, O Lord, not unto us, but unto thy name give glory, for thy mercy, and for thy truth's sake."

We should praise God for His righteousness.

<u>Psalm 35:28</u>

"And my tongue shall speak of thy righteousness and of thy praise all the day long."

We should praise God for His Word.

<u>Psalm 56:10</u>

"In God will I praise his word: in the Lord will I praise his word."

Praise is the foundation for effective prayers, and the very purpose for our prayers has to be with the final end of praising God. We should praise God every day for who He is and what He is doing in our lives. As we begin our prayers, we should do so with words of praise.

Confession

To confess before God is to be in agreement with what God says about a particular situation. When we confess our sins, we restore our fellowship, or relationship, with God. Confession is also called cleansing. In order to be cleansed, we must first acknowledge our sins before God. To acknowledge means to accept or come to a clear understanding and agreement about a particular situation. God wants us to admit our sins before Him. If we deny our sins, we are really deceiving ourselves. This is an indication that the truth is not in us.

Psalm 32:5

"I acknowledged my sin unto thee, and mine iniquity have I not hid. I said, I will confess my transgressions unto the Lord; and thou forgavest the iniquity of my sin."

1 John 1:10

"If we say that we have not sinned, we make him a liar, and his word is not in us."

We need to agree with what God's Word says about our sin condition. As we agree in prayer, we should talk with God about our sin problem. We have God's promise that if we confess our sins, He is faithful and just to forgive us and cleanse us from all unrighteousness.

1 John 1:9

"If we confess our sins, he is faithful and just to forgive us our sins, and to cleanse us from all unrighteousness."

If our heart is blameless, we are assured that God will hear our prayers. Our personal life has to be pure. If we pray without confessing our sins, God will not hear our prayers.

Psalm 66:18

"If I regard iniquity in my heart, the Lord will not hear me."

Micah 3:4

"Then shall they cry unto the Lord, but he will not hear them: he will even hide his face from them at that time, as they have behaved themselves ill in their doings."

Therefore, in order for our prayers to be effective, we have to confess our sins to God. If we do not confess our sins, our prayers may be in vain; God may not answer.

Isaiah 59:2

"But your iniquities have separated between you and your God, and your sins have hid his face from you, that he will not hear."

Our God is all-holy. He hates sin. He wants us to be cleansed as we come before Him in prayer. As we confess our sins, we should desire for God to create in us a new heart, or cleanse us by His creative power. This cleansing will place us in a right relationship with God.

Psalm 51:10

"Create in me a clean heart, O God; and renew a right spirit within me."

We must ask forgiveness for sins both known and unknown.

Matthew 6:12

"And forgive us our debts, as we forgive our debtors."

Intercession

To intercede means to pray on behalf of others. Our Lord Jesus is always praying on our behalf. We have access to the throne of God only because of the intercessory prayer of our High Priest Christ Jesus.

Hebrews 7:25

> *"Wherefore he is able also to save them to the uttermost that come unto God by him, seeing he ever liveth to make intercession for them."*

As our Lord is interceding on our behalf, He is calling us to intercede for others. Through the prayer of intercession, souls can be saved. Our prayers can also change circumstances. Our Lord exhorts us to not only pray for all men but also to pray for kings and all in authority.

1 Timothy 2:1

> *"I exhort therefore, that, first of all, supplications, prayers, intercessions, and giving of thanks, be made for all men."*

Moses is one of the most well-known intercessors to Christians. Moses prayed on behalf of his people. We must also stand in the gap for others and intercede on behalf of sinful men.

Exodus 32:31-32

> *"And Moses returned unto the Lord, and said, Oh, this people have sinned a great sin, and have made them gods of gold. Yet now, if thou*

wilt forgive their sin—; and if not, blot me, I pray thee, out of thy book which thou hast written."

How should we intercede? First, make a list of needs. Divide the list into sections. For example, needs for family, for church, for the country, and for missionaries. Each day, pray through the list. As prayers are answered, give thanks to God for answering. As you make a new list each week, add new needs. The list can also be divided by days of the week. That is, on different days, intercede for different groups of needs. For example:

Sunday:	*Intercede for those in need of salvation.*
Monday:	*Intercede for family and friends.*
Tuesday:	*Intercede for the church (local and worldwide).*
Wednesday:	*Intercede for the government.*
Thursday:	*Intercede for the community.*
Friday:	*Intercede for coworkers.*
Saturday:	*Intercede for those with special needs.*

Petition

Petition means asking God for personal things. Our Father in heaven wants us to relate to Him as sons and daughters. Therefore, we should have confidence when we come to our Father's throne that God will hear our prayers.

<u>Romans 8:14-17</u>

"For as many as are led by the Spirit of God, they are the sons of God. For ye have not received the spirit of bondage again to fear; but ye have

> received the Spirit of adoption, whereby we cry, Abba, Father. The Spirit itself beareth witness with our spirit, that we are the children of God: And if children, then heirs; heirs of God, and joint-heirs with Christ; if so be that we suffer with him, that we may be also glorified together."

"Praying in Jesus'" name means praying according to His will, prayer by faith in the authority of our Lord Jesus, and giving Him all of the praise and glory. In John 14:14 we are told, "If ye shall ask any thing in my name, I will do it."

John 14:14

> "If ye shall ask any thing in my name, I will do it."

Pray for the Holy Spirit's help. Often we don't know what we should pray for, so we should ask for the Spirit's help.

Romans 8:26

> "Likewise the Spirit also helpeth our infirmities: for we know not what we should pray for as we ought: but the Spirit itself maketh intercession for us with groanings which cannot be uttered."

Pray to understand God's Word.

Psalm 119:12

> "Blessed art thou, O Lord: teach me thy statutes."

Pray for cleansing.

Psalm 51:10

"Create in me a clean heart, O God; and renew a right spirit within me."

Pray that your words and thoughts are acceptable to God.

Psalm 19:14

"Let the words of my mouth, and the meditation of my heart, be acceptable in thy sight, O Lord, my strength, and my redeemer."

Pray for God's guidance.

Psalm 31:3

"For thou art my rock and my fortress; therefore for thy name's sake lead me, and guide me."

Pray for strength.

Psalm 138:3

"In the day when I cried thou answeredst me, and strengthenedst me with strength in my soul."

REVIEW

What is prayer?

Prayer is talking with God.

What does "intercession" mean?

Intercession means to pray for another.

When we present our bodies as a living sacrifice, how are we responding to God?

Presenting our bodies as a living sacrifice to God is our spiritual act of worship.

What does "hallow" mean?

Hallow means to be in reverence and awe of God's holiness.

What is praise?

Praise is the vocal adoration of God.

What does it mean to offer up sacrifices of praise?

Offering up prayer sacrifices refers to those times when we praise God despite the difficult trials we are experiencing.

What do the names of God reveal?

God's names reveal His attributes and character.

What does it mean to praise God because He is God?

Praising God because He is God, means praising God for His name, His righteousness, His Word, and His mighty acts.

What does it mean to confess?

To confess means to agree with what God says about our sins.

What does it mean to acknowledge?

To acknowledge means to admit what is true.

What promise has God made to us if we confess our sins?

If we confess our sins to God, He promises to forgive us of our sins and to cleanse us from all unrighteousness.

What two things should we do in our prayer of confession?

When we confess our sins to God, we should cry out for forgiveness and for cleansing, or divine holiness.

How does "unconfessed" sin affect us?

Unconfessed sin causes God not to hear our prayers.

What does "intercede" mean?

To intercede means to pray on behalf of others.

What is the present function of our Lord Christ Jesus?

Christ Jesus is our eternal intercessor.

Who should we intercede for?

We are commanded to pray for all men.

What does "petition" mean?

Petition means praying for personal things.

How does our Father see us?

Our Father sees us as sons.

What does it mean to pray in Jesus' name?

To pray in Jesus' name means to pray according to His will, wanting to glorify Him, and having faith in His authority.

What are some areas for petition?

Our petitions should include asking the Holy Spirit to help us pray, help us to understand God's Word, to cleanse us from sin, to keep our words and thoughts acceptable, to guide us, and to strengthen us.

Chapter 10

Giving

It is a blessing to believers to give to the work and the needs of the church. Giving is a blessing from God and a joyous privilege. As God's children, we should always give. God gave His son to die for our sins that we might have eternal life. We, therefore, should desire to give also. This chapter covers the steps that must be taken in order to serve God through our giving.

The Principles of Giving

Give of Yourself

Before we can give our resources to the Lord and our fellow man, we must first learn to give of our own self. God has commanded us to present, or give, ourselves to Him for His service. Our money is not an acceptable substitute for ourselves. God has more than enough treasure in heaven to take care of all; and He is the provider of all that we have.

Romans 12:1

"I beseech you therefore, brethren, by the mercies of God, that ye present your bodies a living sacrifice, holy, acceptable unto God, which is your reasonable service."

Give a Tithe

The word "tithe" means "one-tenth" and refers to the practice of giving one-tenth of our income to the Lord. Many people claim that the law of tithing is of the Old Testament and not for today. While today we are not under the law of the Old Testament, we are certainly under grace. Grace demands giving more—not less. Therefore, if someone has a problem with tithing, he should give more, not less. The fact that we are under grace and not under the law is not an excuse to neglect giving. As God's children, we should give above and beyond that which was required under Old Testament tithing. We should also give willingly and cheerfully.

2 Corinthians 9:7

"Every man according as he purposeth in his heart, so let him give; not grudgingly, or of necessity: for God loveth a cheerful giver."

Give to the Needs of Fellow Saints

Not only should we give of ourselves to God, but we should also dedicate ourselves to ministering to our fellow saints in Christ. This involves not only giving faithfully to support the ministry of the church, but also to those who are in need. When we give to God's saints, we know that we are doing what is pleasing to God.

2 Corinthians 8:5

"And this they did, not as we hoped, but first gave their own selves to the Lord, and unto us by the will of God."

Give in Proportion to Your Blessings

Christians should give in proportion to the blessings they have received from God. It is not the amount of the gift that God respects but the desire of the person giving the gift. As we earn greater income, we should increase our giving to God. We should also establish a regular schedule for our giving.

1 Corinthians 16:2

"Upon the first day of the week let every one of you lay by him in store, as God hath prospered him, that there be no gatherings when I come."

2 Corinthians 8:12

"For if there be first a willing mind, it is accepted according to that a man hath, and not according to that he hath not."

Give Sacrificially

In the following Scripture, the mite was the smallest of copper coins and its worth very little. Others were giving in abundance. Yet our Lord said that this widow gave more than anyone. Her giving was more acceptable to God because she gave sacrificially. She gave all that she had. She gave her whole livelihood. We too should give sacrificially. Often, people give out of their excess, but God is not pleased with such giving. Remember that we can never out-give God. God blesses us as we give.

> *Mark 12:42-44*
>
> *"And there came a certain poor widow, and she threw in two mites, which make a farthing. And he called unto him his disciples, and saith unto them, Verily I say unto you, That this poor widow hath cast more in, than all they which have cast into the treasury: For all they did cast in of their abundance; but she of her want did cast in all that she had, even all her living."*

Give Willingly and Cheerfully

Even though we are commanded to give, God does not want believers to give solely as an obligation. God wants us to prayerfully consider our gift, and then give it cheerfully. We should never regret a gift that we gave to the Lord. All believers should consider giving a ministry.

> *2 Corinthians 9:7*
>
> *"Every man according as he purposeth in his heart, so let him give; not grudgingly, or of necessity: for God loveth a cheerful giver."*

Give to Meet Specific Needs

Apart from regular tithing, we should give as special needs arise. We must be swift to give to the needs of believers as they become known to us. These gifts can be made directly to those in need. Gifts given to meet special needs are pleasing to the Lord.

> *1 John 3:17*
>
> *"But whoso hath this world's good, and seeth his brother have need, and shutteth up his bowels of compassion from him, how dwelleth the love of God in him?"*

Financial Stewardship

In order to give effectively, we have to understand the biblical principles of financial stewardship. If we do not handle our finances properly, we will not be able to minister effectively in our giving. This section provides some basic principles we can use in handling our finances in a way that is pleasing to God.

Greed

Satan tempts believers through the desires of their hearts. He tempts men to lust for riches. As God's children, we have to seek those things which are above. We have to seek first the kingdom of God. Loving money and material things will cause us to stray from the faith. God wants us to trust fully in Him for everything. He will supply our needs. We have to safeguard our hearts from Satan's attacks.

> *1 Timothy 6:9-10*
>
> *"But they that will be rich fall into temptation and a snare, and into many foolish and hurtful lusts, which drown men in destruction and perdition. For the love of money is the root of all evil:*

which while some coveted after, they have erred from the faith, and pierced themselves through with many sorrows."

Financial Planning

Finances must be planned with godly wisdom. The manner in which we handle our finances reflects our spiritual condition. God wants us to handle money and other material possessions in a manner that glorifies Him. We should pray for the Holy Spirit to guide us in spending our money. This matter is of such importance to God that He has told us that in order for us to be spiritually responsible, we must also be financially responsible.

Luke 16:11

"If therefore ye have not been faithful in the unrighteous mammon, who will commit to your trust the true riches?"

<u>*James 4:13-15*</u>

"Go to now, ye that say, Today or to morrow we will go into such a city, and continue there a year, and buy and sell, and get gain: Whereas ye know not what shall be on the morrow. For what is your life? It is even a vapor, that appeareth for a little time, and then vanisheth away. For that ye ought to say, If the Lord will, we shall live, and do this, or that."

Sharing with Others

We must care for our fellow saints by being sensitive to one another's needs. We should also pray that God will use us to support one another. We should be swift to give to others who are in need. God is pleased when we share, especially when we do so sacrificially. What happens when God's children who have but do not share with others? They become haughty and grow to trust more in their own riches and less in the omnipotent power of God.

Hebrews 13:16

"But to do good and to communicate forget not: for with such sacrifices God is well pleased."

1 Timothy 6:17-18

"Charge them that are rich in this world, that they be not highminded, nor trust in uncertain riches, but in the living God, who giveth us richly all things to enjoy; That they do good, that they be rich in good works, ready to distribute, willing to communicate."

Proverbs 3:27-28

"Withhold not good from them to whom it is due, when it is in the power of thine hand to do it. Say not unto thy neighbor, Go, and come again, and tomorrow I will give; when thou hast it by thee."

Your Family's Needs

Although God exhorts us to give to our fellow saints and others, He expects us to provide for our household. This responsibility must be our first priority. Certainly this does not mean trying to do so by our own strength and ability. We have to pray and depend on our Lord. We can meet this responsibility through Christ who strengthens us. The believer who does not seek to fulfill this responsibility is worse than an unbeliever.

1 Timothy 5:8

"But if any provide not for his own, and specially for those of his own house, he hath denied the faith, and is worse than an infidel."

Savings

A believer who is seeking to grow spiritually will not become concerned with laying up treasures on earth. This does not mean that believers should not save money for future needs, but it does mean that God's children should not place their trust in earthly wealth. Wealth can lead to pride and over self-reliance instead of the Holy Spirit's guidance. We should trust in God for everything. He will supply our needs according to His riches in glory by Christ Jesus (Philip. 4:19). We should keep our minds on things that pertain to heaven.

Philippians 4:19

"But my God shall supply all your need according to his riches in glory by Christ Jesus."

Matthew 6:19-20

"Lay not up for yourselves treasures upon earth, where moth and rust doth corrupt, and where thieves break through and steal: But lay up for yourselves treasures in heaven, where neither moth nor rust doth corrupt, and where thieves do not break through nor steal."

2 Corinthians. 4:18

"While we look not at the things which are seen, but at the things which are not seen: for the things which are seen are temporal; but the things which are not seen are eternal."

The final destiny of the believer's life is heaven. Everything on earth will one day perish. Only those things that count for heaven will last. Only those things that bring spiritual rewards are worth seeking after. We should place priority on our possessions in heaven and seek those things that will strengthen us spiritually. This will cause us to view our material possessions with a pure heart and to not become overly concerned with earthly matters.

Possessions

Possessions do not bring fulfillment and contentment. Material possessions will not bring peace and joy. Peace and joy come from doing God's will. Life's purpose and fulfillment cannot be achieved by accumulating material possessions. In this materialistic age, God reminds us that we need to be looking to Jesus, the Perfecter of our faith. Nothing in this world will satisfy our spiritual need. This is why our Lord Jesus told us to seek first the kingdom of God and His righteousness and all that we need will be added to us (Matt. 6:33).

> *Matthew 6:33*
>
> *"But seek ye first the kingdom of God, and his righteousness; and all these things shall be added unto you."*
>
> *Luke 12:15*
>
> *"And he said unto them, Take heed, and beware of covetousness: for a man's life consisteth not in the abundance of the things which he possesseth."*

REVIEW

What does "tithe" mean?

Tithe means "one-tenth" and refers to the Old Testament practice of giving "one-tenth" of one's income to the Lord.

What does it mean to give of ourselves?

"Giving of ourselves to God" means presenting ourselves before God for His service. It means dedicating ourselves and our resources to the Lord.

How should believers view their responsibility for giving?

Believers should think of giving as a privilege made possible by God's grace. Christ willingly gave His life for our sins, and we should, out of love and gratitude, follow His example.

Apart from tithing, how should we give?

We should give as special needs arise.

What should be the attitude of our heart when we give?

We should give cheerfully and not grudgingly.

What is the effect of the love of money?

The effect of the love of money is the root of all evil and stirs up lust for sin.

How does Satan attack us in relationship to riches?

Satan tempts man to lust for money and material wealth.

What promise has God made us in regard to our needs?

As we seek to do God's will, God will supply our needs according to His riches in glory by Christ Jesus.

How does God want us to handle money and other material possessions?

God wants us to handle our money and other material possessions in a manner that glorifies His name.

What does it mean to give sacrificially?

Sacrificial giving means giving cheerfully when we ourselves have needs.

What command has been given to those who are rich?

God warns believers not to become haughty or to trust in uncertain riches; they should trust in the living God.

How should we view our families' needs?

Believers must provide for the needs of their families before they provide for others. If we do not minister to our family, we are acting worse than unbelievers.

As God's children, where should we set our minds?

Believers should set their minds on those things that pertain to heaven.

What will bring "life's fulfillment"?

Life's fulfillment can only be achieved by looking to Jesus, the Author and Perfecter of our faith.

Chapter 11

Bible Study

There is a very important reason why a believer should study the Bible. The Bible, which is the Word of God, instructs us on the principles of Christianity. In order for us to grow spiritually, we must study the Bible. Our faith grows through our knowledge of God's Word. Understanding God's Word helps us to understand God's purpose for our lives. The Bible also teaches us about Satan and the spiritual warfare being waged between him and believers. We should not be ignorant of the devices of the enemy. Therefore, Bible study is vital to our well-being.

Reasons for Studying the Bible

There are numerous reasons why Christians must study the Bible. This section covers the various areas that the Word of God touches.

The Word of God saves us from the practice of sin.

The Bible speaks not only of the fact that we are set free from the penalty of sin, that is, eternity in hell, but also from the practice of sin. The Word of God works a change in those who truly want to serve God. When we hide the Word of God in our hearts, we are able to resist sin.

James 1:21

"Wherefore lay apart all filthiness and superfluity of naughtiness, and receive with meekness the engrafted word, which is able to save your souls."

Psalm 119:11

"Thy word have I hid in mine heart, that I might not sin against thee."

The Word of God gives us true knowledge of God and victory over Satan.

God reveals Himself through His Word. Studying the Bible gives us the knowledge of the truth that can set us free from the power of sin and death. This knowledge also enables us to be victorious in our battle with Satan.

1 John 2:13

"I write unto you, fathers, because ye have known him that is from the beginning. I write unto you, young men, because ye have overcome the wicked one. I write unto you, little children, because ye have known the Father."

James 4:6-8a

"But he giveth more grace. Wherefore he saith, God resisteth the proud, but giveth grace unto

the humble. Submit yourselves therefore to God. Resist the devil, and he will flee from you. Draw nigh to God, and he will draw nigh to you."

<u>John 8:32</u>

"And ye shall know the truth, and the truth shall make you free."

The Word of God enables us to experience fullness of joy.

Joy is a fruit of the Holy Spirit that is produced when the seed of God's Word is planted in our hearts (Gal. 5:22-23a).

<u>Galatians 5:22-23a</u>

"But the fruit of the Spirit is love, joy, peace, longsuffering, gentleness, goodness, faith, Meekness, temperance."

<u>1 John 1:4</u>

"And these things write we unto you, that your joy may be full."

<u>John 16:24</u>

"Hitherto have ye asked nothing in my name: ask, and ye shall receive, that your joy may be full."

The Word of God enables us to know the truth.

The Bible is the source of all truth and is the standard by which we can discern what is true and what is false.

Acts 17:11

"These were more noble than those in Thessalonica, in that they received the word with all readiness of mind, and searched the scriptures daily, whether those things were so."

2 Timothy 2:15

"Study to show thyself approved unto God, a workman that needeth not to be ashamed, rightly dividing the word of truth."

The Word of God gives us the ability to discern good and evil.

Those who study and obey the Word of God gain the ability to discern good and evil. This ability to discern good and evil increases as one increases his diligence in the study of God's Word.

Hebrews 5:13-14

"For every one that useth milk is unskillful in the word of righteousness: for he is a babe. But strong meat belongeth to them that are of full age, even those who by reason of use have their senses exercised to discern both good and evil."

The Word of God convicts us of sin.

The Word of God penetrates deep into the soul of man. It exposes and reveals the very intent of the heart.

> *Hebrews 4:12*
>
> *"For the Word of God is quick, and powerful, and sharper than any two-edged sword, piercing even to the dividing asunder of soul and spirit, and of the joints and marrow, and is a discerner of the thoughts and intents of the heart."*

The Word of God equips us for doing good works.

> *2 Timothy 3:16-17*
>
> *"All Scripture is given by inspiration of God, and is profitable for doctrine, for reproof, for correction, for instruction in righteousness: That the man of God may be perfect, thoroughly furnished unto all good works."*

The Word of God accomplishes four main purposes:

It teaches sound doctrine. Sound doctrine is truth concerning the revelation of God. The Bible shows us the path we need to follow. It teaches us the right way to live.

It reproves us of sin. A reproof shows us where we have gone wrong. Its purpose is to lead us to repentance.

It instructs us on how to correct our wrong steps.

It shows us how to avoid sin and live righteously.

The Word of God is our manual for life. It reveals how the Christian should live. It is important to trust the Word of God for accomplishing God's purposes in our life.

Isaiah 55:10-11

"For as the rain cometh down, and the snow from heaven, and returneth not thither, but watereth the earth, and maketh it bring forth and bud, that it may give seed to the sower, and bread to the eater: So shall my word be that goeth forth out of my mouth: it shall not return unto me void, but it shall accomplish that which I please, and it shall prosper in the thing whereto I sent it."

Keys to Effective Bible Study

Bible study is essential for our spiritual growth. If we do not study the Bible, Satan will establish strongholds in our lives. Attending church is no substitute for personal Bible study. Although God commands us "not to neglect the assembling of ourselves together," it is God's Word that is the spiritual food that causes us to grow. Bible study produces a level of spiritual growth that cannot be attained by any other means. The Bible tells us that we should desire the Word of God like a newborn baby desires milk. Bible study is our spiritual food. Just as we need physical food to live, so we also need spiritual food to grow spiritually.

1 Peter 2:2

"As newborn babes, desire the sincere milk of the word, that ye may grow thereby."

Bible study is also the time when we meet with God. Our heavenly Father seeks our fellowship. He wants us to know Him the way He is declaring Himself through His Word. Through Bible study, we express our love for God and our desire to serve Him. To desire God's Word is to worship

Him. It is to adore Him. The Word of God brings joy and rejoicing in our hearts.

Jeremiah 15:16

"Thy words were found, and I did eat them; and thy word was unto me the joy and rejoicing of mine heart: for I am called by thy name, O Lord God of hosts."

It takes discipline and determination to develop a healthy personal Bible study. It means taking time from your busy schedule to study. Bible study is more than a hobby; it is a spiritual necessity. Recognizing the importance of Bible study helps us to put first things first. We sometimes have to give up something in order to be successful in Bible study. Faithful and fruitful Bible study requires much discipline to become a healthy spiritual habit.

1 Timothy 4:13.

"Till I come, give attendance to reading, to exhortation, to doctrine."

2 Timothy 2:15

"Study to show thyself approved unto God, a workman that needeth not to be ashamed, rightly dividing the word of truth."

The Bible tells us that the Bereans searched the Scriptures daily. We too should have daily Bible study, preferably at a definite time every day. This time can be brief in the beginning but should lengthen as we grow in God's Word. If too much is attempted too quickly, it can lead to discouragement. Therefore, pray and trust that God will grant you the grace to regularly study the Bible.

> *Acts 17:11*
>
> "These were more noble than those in Thessalonica, in that they received the word with all readiness of mind, and searched the Scriptures daily, whether those things were so."

A Quiet Spirit

We live in a world of great noise. If we are too noisy, we will not be able to hear the voice of the Spirit, so we must learn to be quiet in our soul.

> *Psalms 46:10a*
>
> "Be still, and know that I am God."
>
> *Isaiah 30:15*
>
> "...in quietness and in confidence shall be your strength..."

Each time we read a portion of Scripture, our hearts should be open to the Holy Spirit ministering God's truth to us.

If we are weary physically, we may not be as alert as we need to be in order to receive the fullness of God's Word. If we desire to get up early in the morning to enjoy a good or fulfilling time of Bible study, it is imperative that we get to bed early. We should always be aware of our physical condition.

Revelation 1:3

"Blessed is he that readeth, and they that hear the words of this prophecy, and keep those things which are written therein: for the time is at hand."

God has promised us that He will bless us as we read His Word. We may not always understand everything as we read, but just as we expect God to answer our prayers, we should expect God to bless us through His Word. We should ask the Holy Spirit to help us understand God's Word and cause us to know our Lord Christ Jesus and the power of His resurrection and the fellowship of His suffering.

Ephesians 3:20

"Now unto him that is able to do exceeding abundantly above all that we ask or think, according to the power that worketh in us."

God's blessings are far beyond what we can even think or imagine. Our God works supernaturally in our lives. He declares His omnipotence. He is all-powerful and all authority has been given to our Lord Christ Jesus.

The Benefits of Bible Study

A person who studies the Bible sees himself for who he is, just as a mirror reflects a person's physical image. He learns exactly where he stands with God. However, if he does not heed the Bible, he is like a foolish man who looks at himself in the mirror and then forgets what he looks like.

James 1:23

"*For if any be a hearer of the word, and not a doer, he is like unto a man beholding his natural face in a glass.*"

Evil will never prevail against God's will. The Word of God reveals truth, exposes evil, and equips us to discern the truth. It is the knowledge of God's Word that defeats Satan's evil devices.

Jeremiah 23:29

"*Is not my word like as a fire? saith the Lord; and like a hammer that breaketh the rock in pieces?*"

When we first believed the Gospel, we received eternal life and became entirely new creatures. This new life is spoken of in the same terms as a natural human is conceived and born. Spiritually, we are begotten with God's very seed, which is the Word of God, and born again into eternal life.

1 Peter 1:23

"*Being born again, not of corruptible seed, but of incorruptible, by the Word of God, which liveth and abideth for ever.*"

James 1:18

"*Of his own will begat he us with the word of truth, that we should be a kind of firstfruits of his creatures.*"

The Word of God has the power to cleanse us from the practice of sin because it deals with the heart, rooting out evil desires and creating in us a love of God and a desire to do His will.

Ephesians 5:26

"That he might sanctify and cleanse it with the washing of water by the word."

John 17:17

"Sanctify them through thy truth: thy word is truth."

Man is naturally blind to spiritual truth. Because the Bible is God's revelation of Himself, it is the only means by which we can learn truth. It is also God's means for communicating His will. Bible study gives us wisdom concerning God's will and plan for our lives.

Psalm 119:105

"Thy word is a lamp unto my feet, and a light unto my path."

Bible study brings about spiritual maturity, or the ability to discern good from evil. It is absolutely necessary for spiritual growth.

1 Peter 2:2

"As newborn babes, desire the sincere milk of the word, that ye may grow thereby."

2 Peter 3:18

"But grow in grace, and in the knowledge of our Lord and Savior Jesus Christ. To him be glory both now and for ever. Amen."

A believer who is spiritually hungry will, through diligent Bible study, be filled with the knowledge of God. He will be satisfied and filled with joy and contentment.

Matthew 4:4

"But he answered and said, It is written, Man shall not live by bread alone, but by every word that proceedeth out of the mouth of God."

Matthew 5:6

"Blessed are they which do hunger and thirst after righteousness: for they shall be filled."

God guarantees us that His Word will produce fruit in our lives much like rain and snow refresh the parched ground and vitalize seeds to grow.

Isaiah 55:10-12

"For as the rain cometh down, and the snow from heaven, and returneth not thither, but watereth the earth, and maketh it bring forth and bud, that it may give seed to the sower, and bread to the eater: So shall my word be that goeth forth out of my mouth: it shall not return unto me void, but it shall accomplish that which I please, and it shall prosper in the

> *thing whereto I sent it. For ye shall go out with joy, and be led forth with peace: the mountains and the hills shall break forth before you into singing, and all the trees of the field shall clap their hands."*

The Word of God equips us to do spiritual battle. It reveals truth and exposes evil, spoiling the devices of Satan and defeating his purposes.

> <u>Ephesians 6:17</u>
>
> *"And take the helmet of salvation, and the sword of the Spirit, which is the Word of God."*

We were saved through the preaching of the Word of God. God's Word brings people into a right relationship with Him.

> <u>Romans 10:17</u>
>
> *"So then faith cometh by hearing, and hearing by the Word of God."*

REVIEW

Why do we need to study the Bible?

We need to study the Bible so that we can understand and practice the principles of Christianity and grow spiritually.

What does the Word of God do for us who believe it and obey it?

The Word of God saves us from both the penalty and practice of sin.

How does the Word of God help us to overcome the evil one?

The Word of God teaches us how to recognize and defeat the devices of Satan.

What brings fullness of joy?

Fullness of joy comes from knowing Christ as He reveals Himself through His Word.

How does God's Word bring conviction?

God's Word is able to convict because it penetrates deep into the soul of man. It has been described as a two-edged sword that discerns the thoughts and intents of man's heart.

As found in 2 Timothy 3:16, what does the word "doctrine" mean?

Doctrine refers to the truth concerning the revelation of God in His Word. It refers to the teaching of God's Word and showing us the right path.

What does reproof mean?

Reproof is that which convicts us of sin. It shows us where we have fallen off the path of righteousness.

What does correction mean?

Correction teaches us how to right our wrong steps. It shows us how to get back on the right path.

What does "instruction in righteousness" mean?

Instruction in righteousness teaches us how to avoid sin and how to continue to do what is right. It shows us how to stay on the right path.

What assurance does the Scripture give us concerning the accomplishment of the word?

The Bible assures us that the word will accomplish the purpose for which God sent it.

Why does the Word of God minister to us through doctrine, reproof, correction, and instruction?

God's Word ministers to us in these ways so that we may be complete and thoroughly equipped for every good work.

Why is personal Bible study essential?

Personal Bible study is essential because the Word of God is the spiritual food that produces spiritual growth.

How does the Bible describe our desire for the word?

Our desire for the word should be like newborn babies desiring milk.

What are we expressing toward God as we study the Bible?

When we study the Bible, we express our love and worship of God.

How does personal Bible study affect our heart?

Bible study causes us to become more Christlike and to be filled with joy.

What does it mean to be fervent in our personal Bible study?

To be fervent in our Bible study means to take time each day to study God's Word.

What are some healthy practices that can help us to be more fervent in our Bible study?

Set a fixed time and place to study God's Word and give Bible study priority at all times. Be disciplined in studying God's Word and give up those things that might hinder our studying.

How often should we study the Bible?

We should study the Bible daily.

What does it mean to be quiet in spirit?

To be quiet in spirit means to be humble before God and listen to the Holy Spirit as He ministers to us through His Word.

Why should we expect a blessing when we study God's Word?

God has promised us that He will bless us as we read His Word.

Chapter 12

Victory over Satan

Christians are in a spiritual war. The enemy is Satan. Satan's greatest attack against the church is deception. He has even deceived some into believing that he does not exist. Our Lord Jesus exposed Satan as the father of lies. Satan is a liar and a murderer. His aim is to destroy the believer. However, through Christ believers can have victory over Satan.

> *John 8:44*
>
> *"Ye are of your father the devil, and the lusts of your father ye will do. He was a murderer from the beginning, and abode not in the truth, because there is no truth in him. When he speaketh a lie, he speaketh of his own: for he is a liar, and the father of it."*
>
> *1 Corinthians 15:57*
>
> *"But thanks be to God, which giveth us the victory through our Lord Jesus Christ."*

The four keys to victory over Satan are discussed in the following sections.

1. Acknowledge Christ

The first key to victory over Satan is to acknowledge our relationship with Christ. This is done in a number of ways.

Understand that we have been crucified with Christ.

Christ's death set us free from our old sinful nature. Just as Jesus was raised in newness of life, so to we live a new life of faith that is yielded to God and dead to sin. The same power that raised Jesus from the dead empowers believers to stand against Satan.

Galatians 2:20

"I am crucified with Christ: nevertheless I live; yet not I, but Christ liveth in me: and the life which I now live in the flesh I live by the faith of the Son of God, who loved me, and gave himself for me."

Earnestly pursue the knowledge of Christ.

All of our profits and gains will not bring fellowship with God. Material things do not bring inner peace. Therefore, like Paul, we have to consider all things as loss so that we can begin to grow in our knowledge of Christ. The focus of our life should be Christ. We must continually count all we have as loss and thank God each day that the Lordship of Christ is first in our lives.

Philippians 3:7-8

"But what things were gain to me, those I counted loss for Christ. Yea doubtless, and I count all things but loss for the excellency of the knowledge of Christ Jesus my Lord: for whom I have suffered the loss of all things, and do count them but dung, that I may win Christ."

Understand that Christ lives in us.

Christ dwelling in us is a mystery. However, as God's children, the Holy Spirit reveals this mystery to us. We are growing to know the glorious wealth we have in Christ. Christ is the answer to all of our needs. Furthermore, He is our hope. Our future is in Christ's purpose for us. He has His plan for us. We have to accept by faith this mystery being revealed.

Colossians 1:27

"To whom God would make known what is the riches of the glory of this mystery among the Gentiles; which is Christ in you, the hope of glory."

1 Timothy 1:1

"Paul, an apostle of Jesus Christ by the commandment of God our Savior, and Lord Jesus Christ, which is our hope."

The Spirit of Christ dwells in us.

The Holy Spirit first brought us to Christ. Once we become a Christian, the Holy Spirit dwells in us. If the Holy Spirit does not dwell in someone, that person is not saved. The Holy Spirit in us gives us a new life—a life of righteousness. By faith, we have to accept the leading of the Spirit of Christ in us.

> *Romans 8:9-10*
>
> *"But ye are not in the flesh, but in the Spirit, if so be that the Spirit of God dwell in you. Now if any man have not the Spirit of Christ, he is none of his. And if Christ be in you, the body is dead because of sin; but the Spirit is life because of righteousness."*

Christ's love controls us.

It is the love of Christ that was demonstrated on Calvary. God loved us that while we were yet sinners, Christ died for us. Nothing can separate us from the love of Christ. In response to God's love towards us, we should live for Him. Everyday we should express through prayer our gratitude and thankfulness for God's controlling love.

> *2 Corinthians 5:14-15*
>
> *" For the love of Christ constraineth us; because we thus judge, that if one died for all, then were all dead: And that he died for all, that they which live should not henceforth live unto themselves, but unto him which died for them, and rose again."*

Every thought is in obedience to Christ.

Satan wages war in the battlefield of the mind. The mind is where the darts of Satan strike. But praise God, Christ pulls down the strongholds of the mind and sets us free. All of our thoughts come into the obedience of the knowledge of Christ. We have to pray for the Holy Spirit to renew and empower our minds.

<u>2 Corinthians 10:4-5</u>

"(For the weapons of our warfare are not carnal, but mighty through God to the pulling down of strongholds;) Casting down imaginations, and every high thing that exalteth itself against the knowledge of God, and bringing into captivity every thought to the obedience of Christ."

Our relationship with Christ is our first key to victory. Who we are in Christ ensures us of the victory. As a spiritual exercise, give God praise every day for the following:

That we have been crucified with Christ
That we are growing in the knowledge of Christ
That Christ is in us
That the Holy Spirit dwells in us
That Christ's love controls us
That God's power is bringing all of our thoughts to the obedience of Christ

Satan is always trying to lie to us about our relationship with Christ. We have to stand on God's truth. Our God is always giving us the victory because of our relationship with Him.

2. The Holy Spirit

The second key to victory over Satan is the person and work of the Holy Spirit. At the very instant we are saved, we are sealed with the Holy Spirit. This permanent sealing guarantees our salvation.

Ephesians 1:13

"In whom ye also trusted, after that ye heard the word of truth, the Gospel of your salvation: in whom also after that ye believed, ye were sealed with that Holy Spirit of promise."

Our Lord Jesus promised us that the Holy Spirit would empower us to be witnesses to the Gospel message.

Acts 1:8

"But ye shall receive power, after that the Holy Ghost is come upon you: and ye shall be witnesses unto me both in Jerusalem, and in all Judea, and in Samaria, and unto the uttermost part of the earth."

As God's children we have this heavenly power working through us; God's Holy Spirit building the church and destroying the work of Satan. Satan attacks believers in two ways: through the flesh and through our members (our eyes, our minds, and other members). Satan wants us to walk in the flesh. However, the Holy Spirit empowers us to walk in the Spirit and not in the flesh, giving us the victory over Satan.

Galatians 5:16-17

"This I say then, Walk in the Spirit, and ye shall not fulfill the lust of the flesh. For the flesh lusteth against the Spirit, and the Spirit against the flesh: and these are contrary the one to the other: so that ye cannot do the things that ye would."

To walk in the Spirit means to be energized by the power of the Spirit. It also means to be under the divine direction of the Holy Spirit. Both Satan and the Spirit are battling for the soul of the believer. As we yield to the Holy Spirit's control, we will experience what is meant to walk in the Spirit.

Perhaps the attack on the flesh is Satan's greatest onslaught against believes, and is often where the believer loses the battle. This is because the flesh is weak. The Bible describes the flesh as the dwelling place of no good thing. Paul explains that the flesh, which is the sinful nature, causes us to sin.

Romans 7:16-20

"If then I do that which I would not, I consent unto the law that it is good. Now then it is no more I that do it, but sin that dwelleth in me. For I know that in me (that is, in my flesh,) dwelleth no good thing: for to will is present with me; but how to perform that which is good I find not. For the good that I would I do not: but the evil which I would not, that I do. Now if I do that I would not, it is no more I that do it, but sin that dwelleth in me."

How should the believer respond to the flesh? We should have no confidence in it. We should expect nothing from the flesh. The flesh is sinful. It does not matter what we do with the flesh. It is still the sinful nature. Some people try to educate the flesh and others try to reform it, but it is to no avail. The Bible tells us that anyone who is in the flesh cannot please God.

Philippians 3:3

"For we are the circumcision, which worship God in the spirit, and rejoice in Christ Jesus, and have no confidence in the flesh."

Romans 8:8

"So then they that are in the flesh cannot please God."

Steps can be taken to guard against Satan's attacks against the flesh:

Make no provision for the flesh.

To "put on Christ" means to accept the Lordship of Christ in your life by faith.

Romans 13:14

"But put ye on the Lord Jesus Christ, and make not provision for the flesh, to fulfill the lusts thereof."

Yield yourself to God.

You have to resist allowing your members (that is your eyes, your mind, your hand, and all other members) to be instruments of unrighteousness. Instead, yield your members as instruments of righteousness. Think good thoughts. Look at things that are pleasing to God. Whatever you do, do it to glorify God.

Romans 6:13

"Neither yield ye your members as instruments of unrighteousness unto sin: but yield yourselves unto God, as those that are alive from the dead, and your members as instruments of righteousness unto God."

3. The Power of Prayer

The third key to the believer's victory over Satan is prayer. Prayer is the believer's strongest weapon against Satan. Through prayer, the believer becomes an instrument in God's hand. Prayer also enables us to experience the mighty power of the Holy Spirit working through us. As we pray, we become a formidable opponent to the power of darkness. Satan does not want us to pray. He knows that when we pray, he loses the battle and he must flee under the authority of God's Word.

Pray in the Spirit.

The battle for our souls is fought in the realm of prayer. It is in this realm that we have the victory. To pray effectively, we must pray in the Spirit, under the control of the Holy Spirit. We don't know how to pray so the Spirit Himself intercedes for us in accordance with God's will and guides us in our prayers.

Romans 8:26-27

"Likewise the Spirit also helpeth our infirmities: for we know not what we should pray for as we ought: but the Spirit itself maketh intercession for us with groanings which cannot be uttered. And he that searcheth the hearts knoweth what is the mind of the Spirit, because he maketh intercession for the saints according to the will of God."

Pray in agreement with God's Word.

As we pray, we should do so in agreement with God's Word, which comes from the Holy Spirit. If our prayer is to be in harmony with the Spirit, it must be based on the Word of God. The Holy Spirit guided men to write the Holy Scriptures. As we pray according to God's Word, we can be sure that we are praying in agreement with the Spirit. Our prayers should always be tested by the Word of God.

2 Peter 1:20-21

"Knowing this first, that no prophecy of the scripture is of any private interpretation. For the prophecy came not in old time by the will of man: but holy men of God spake as they were moved by the Holy Ghost."

Pray for protection.

As believers in Christ, our battles are against Satan. Our Lord Jesus is always giving us the victory, but we must claim the victory. Our victory is based on the death, burial, and resurrection of our Lord Christ Jesus.

1 Corinthians 15:57

"But thanks be to God, which giveth us the victory through our Lord Jesus Christ."

In the Gospel of Luke, our Lord Jesus employed this prayer of protection while praying for Peter.

Luke 22:31-32

"And the Lord said, Simon, Simon, behold, Satan hath desired to have you, that he may sift you as wheat: But I have prayed for thee, that thy faith fail not: and when thou art converted, strengthen thy brethren."

4. Intercessory Prayer

The fourth key to victory is prayer for others. Our Lord Jesus wants us to stand in the gap for others through prayer. Satan blinds the unsaved because he does not want them to experience redemption. This is spiritual warfare. God wants us to stand in this gap for others through our prayers.

As we yield to the Holy Spirit, God will use us to intercede for others—to pray for the protection of others. Our Lord Jesus is our High Priest who is always praying for us. God wants to protect us. He wants to keep us. He wants to preserve us blameless until He comes for us.

1 Thessalonians 5:23

"And the very God of peace sanctify you wholly; and I pray God your whole spirit and soul and body be preserved blameless unto the coming of our Lord Jesus Christ."

Satan often uses the presence of evil items or practices to hinder our prayers, so it is important that we cleanse evil from our homes and our lives. God instructed Israel to burn all of their images of false gods. There may be items believers have at home that they are not aware of that contain evil meanings. Therefore, ask the Holy Spirit for discernment and do a house cleaning.

<u>Deuteronomy 7:25-26</u>

"The graven images of their gods shall ye burn with fire: thou shalt not desire the silver or gold that is on them, nor take it unto thee, lest thou be snared therein: for it is an abomination to the Lord thy God. Neither shalt thou bring an abomination into thine house, lest thou be a cursed thing like it: but thou shalt utterly detest it, and thou shalt utterly abhor it; for it is a cursed thing.

REVIEW

Who is our enemy?

Our enemy is Satan.

Who does our Lord expose Satan to be?

Our Lord exposes Satan as the father of lies.

What happens in our relationship with the Holy Spirit once we are saved?

At the instant we are saved, we are sealed with the Holy Spirit.

What does the seal of the Holy Spirit signify?

The seal of the Holy Spirit signifies that we belong to God for all eternity.

In serving as witnesses for Christ, who is our source of power?

Our source of power is the person of the Holy Spirit.

As God's children, how should we walk?

We should walk in the Spirit.

What does it mean to walk in the Spirit?

To walk in the Spirit means to be led by the Holy Spirit. Walking in the Spirit means we allow Him to control and lead us.

What does Satan use to attack the believer?

Satan uses the flesh to attack the believer.

How should the believer view the flesh?

Believers should have no confidence in the flesh.

How should the believer respond to Satan's attack against his flesh?

Believers should make no provision for the flesh and should yield to the Holy Spirit.

Select Scripture Reference Index

Genesis
1:27-29 26
3:17-19 26
1:1 30
1:26a 31
15:1-2 34
14:18-20 36
16:13 37
17:1 40
22:13-14 41
22:18 91
3:16 91
6:5 119
3:1-5 248
3:15 286

Exodus
3:13-14 32
15:26 43
17:15 44
34:6 69
32:31-32 344

Leviticus
20:8 45

19:2 61
20:26 61
20:7 257

Numbers
23:19 33
15:40 62

Deuteronomy
31:6 50
33:27a 59
7:9 66
18:15-19 79
4:2 199
12:32 199
7:25-26 392

Joshua
1:9 50

Judges
6:23:-24 47

I Samuel
17:47 33

1:3a....................48	34:15....................39
17:45....................49	34:8-10....................42
15:22-23....................84	84:11....................42
16:1....................84	4:3a....................45
16:12-13....................85	23:1....................52,120
31:7....................291	139:6....................55
	139:7-8....................59
2 Samuel	7:9....................63
7:12-13....................92	86:13a....................64
7:12-13....................122	136:26....................64
7:11b-13....................143	145:8....................65
	145:9....................68
1 Chronicles	2:6-7....................83
16:34....................64	45:6-7....................84
17:11-15....................122	89:3-4....................93
	132:11....................93
2 Chronicles	2:7....................102
16:9a....................38	23:1....................120
5:13-14....................339	2:6-7....................121
	9:7-8....................127
Nehemiah	139:2-4....................136
9:17....................69	46:1....................137
	50:23a....................339
Job	22:3....................340
28:24....................38	115:1....................340
31:4....................38	35:28....................341
34:21....................38	50:10....................341
36:7a....................38	32:5....................342
42:1-6....................58	66:18....................342
33:4....................182	51:10....................343
1:12....................227	119:12....................346
	51:10....................347
Psalm	19:14....................347
13:13-15....................38	31:3....................347
33:18-19....................39	138:3....................347

Proverbs
5:21	39
15:3	39
30:6	200
3:27-28	357

Isaiah
45:22b	31
41:10	51
11:4	63
9:6-7	86
7:14	96
9:6	101
53:5-12	114,118
53:6	118
40:11	120
43:10-11	129
48:12	130
14:12-15	218
59:2	246
4:2	301
65:20	306
2:4	307
2:1-3	307
59:2	343
55:10-11	368
30:15	370
55:10-12	374

Jeremiah
16:17	39
32:19	39
32:18	49
23:5-6	51
23:5-6	85
31:10	120
30:7	283
15:16	369
23:29	372

Lamentations
3:22	65

Ezekiel
48:35	50
34:22-24	121
28:11-12	217
28:15	217
28:13c	218
28:15	227

Daniel
9:25-26	87
7:13-14	104
9:24	283
9:25-26	284
9:27	284
9:27a	287
11:43	288

Joel
2:32	88
2:11	301

Micah
3:4	343

(Preceding entries:)

119:11	364
46:10a	370
119:105	373

Nahum
1:7 68

Zechariah
12:10-11 295
8:23 305

Malachi
3:6a 33,61
3:6a 138

Matthew
28:18 37
19:26 40
6:33 42
28:20 .... 50, 59
19:26 57
28:18 57
1:21 74
16:15-16 76
1:1 91,92
9:27 92
15:22 93
21:9 93
22:41-42 93
1:23 96
1:21 101
26:2 103
26:24 103
9:6 104
16:27 104
24:24 105
24:30 105
24:37 105
24:44 105
25:13 105
25:31 105
26:64 106
28:18 132
8:26 133
14:25-27 133
8:28-32 133
9:4 135
28:20 137
26:38 144
4:2 145
1:21 146
12:28 164
28:19 189
28:18-20 212
12:24 221
13:36-39 234
12:24 237
8:29 239
9:33 240
4:24 241
9:32-33 241
25:41 243
20:28 251
28:18-20 268
24:40-42 274
24:44-46 274
6:10 300
19:28 303
6:9 339
6:12 343
6:19-20 359
6:33 360
4:4 374
5:6 374

Mark

Reference	Page
10:46-47	92
5:7	94
10:45	103
8:31	103
8:38	106
9:9	106
9:12	106
9:31	106
13:26	107
14:21	107
14:41	107
14:62	107
14:27-28	119
12:15	135
10:47	146
13:11	154
3:29-30	162
16:15	189
3:22	221
4:15	231
9:25	238
1:23-24	238
5:2	242
12:42-44	354

Luke

Reference	Page
1:21-33	74
2:21	74
1:32-33	83
2:11	97
19:10	104
9:56	107
9:58	108
12:40	108
17:22	108
17:24	108
17:26-30	108
18:8	109
18:31	109
21:27	109
21:36	109
22:22	110
22:48	110
22:69	110
24:6-7	110
4:35-36	134
5:22	135
6:8	135
11:17	135
12:7	136
1:31	140
1:34-35	140
1:31-33	142
23:46	144
19:41	146
19:10	146
4:14	152, 164
24:49	152
2:27	157
4:1	157
12:11-12	158
2:25-26	159
1:34-35	163
4:18	164
4:1	164
1:35	180
1:34-35	191
11:18	221
10:18	227

8:12	230
8:27-29	242
21:20-24	294
19:11	302
16:11	356
12:15	360
22:31-32	391

John

17:17	23, 46
14:6	25
16:13-15	30
14:1	32
3:16	43
17:17	46
14:27	48
10:11	53
3:16	60
5:24	60
10:11	68
3:16	75
1:41	87
4:25-26	88
3:18	89
11:27	89
1:1	99
1:14	99
3:16-17	101
1:18	102
1:51	110
3:13-15	110
5:27	111
6:27	111
6:53	111
6:62	111
8:28	112
12:23	112
12:34	112
13:31	112
1:29	113
1:36	113
10:11	117
10:14-18	117
3:36	119
10:27-30	119
5:22	124
5:27	126
11:25-26	132
21:17	134
2:25	136
1:18	141
2:25	136
1:18	141
1:14	143
4:6	145
19:28	145
11:35	146
16:13-15	149
15:26	156
16:13a	157
14:26	158
16:14	165
15:26	165
16:8	167
15:5	179
15:16	179
6:63	182
14:30	222
8:44	225
10:10	225

3:36	249	1:5	169
3:16	260	2:4	175
10:28-29	263	4:8	175
3:16	270	4:31	175
14:1-3	318	7:55-56	176
3:36	323	9:17	176
6:40	326	13:52	176
6:44	328	1:8	189
6:65	328	20:28	191
3:3	329	11:27-28	200
1:12-13	330	21:8-9	200
14:14	346	3:2-9	201
8:32	365	19:11-12	202
16:24	365	2:3-6	203
17:17	373	2:4-6	203
8:44	381	2:11b	204
4:12	75	21:8	205
3:22-24	78	20:28	206
7:55-56	112	20:25	208
8:32	115	5:3	231
10:42	126	4:10-12	259
17:31	127	2:1-4	268
2:22	147	1:9-11	293
1:8	152	1:11	295
8:29	155	3:20-21	302
10:19-20	155	3:19	303
13:2	155	7:11	366
8:29	156	17:11	370
10:19-20	156	1:8	386
11:12	156		
16:6-7	157	Romans	
13:4	158	8:8	27
11:28	159	5:8	27
5:9	161	5:12	27
7:51	162	10:9,13	28

5:1 48	3:25 253
5:10-11 48	5:9 254
12:19 49	8:33 254
1:20 56	8:15-17 255
3:21-22 6	3:23 260
3:24-26 65	6:23 261
2:4 69	5:8 261
2:3-4 69	10:9-10 261
10:9,13 88	10:13 262
1:3-4 94	8:38-39 265
5:12-21 95	3:23 269
2:16 127	6:23 269
1:3-4 144	10:9-10 270
15:18-19 152	3:23 321
15:30 153	6:23 322
5:5 153	2:6 322
8:26 155	2:8-9 323
8:11 165	10:9 327
15:7 166	10:10 327
12:6-8 171	10:13 327
8:9b 174	8:14-16 330
12:1 174	12:1 338
12:1-2 178	8:14-17 345
6:13 179	8:26 346
139:7-10 181	12:1 352
12:3-8 196	10:17 375
12:6-7 206	8:9-10 384
12:8a 207	7:16-20 387
12:8b 208,209	8:8 388
3:23 246	13:14 388
6:23 246	6:13 389
5:19 248	8:26-27 390
1:18 249	
1:18 249	I Corinthians
5:19 251	2:14 25

2:10-12	25	12:48	202
2:12	29	14:22a	202
7:22-23	34	15:3.-4	204
15:57	44	5:14	213
1:30	52	11:23	214
1:9	67	11:24-25	214
10:13	67	11:26	215
15:22	95	11:27-28	215
15:45	95	7:5	233
3:8.-15	125	15:21-22	250
4:5	125	6:19-20	251
15:3	141	6:11	256
15:47	147	12:13	264
15:3	148	15:3-4	270
12:13	150	3:11	277
2:11	151	3:12	277
12:11	151	3:13	278
2:10-12	153	3:14-15	278
2:13	158	9:25	278
10:31	166	3:15	281
6:19-20	166	6:2-3	304
6:19	168	15:3	326
3:16	168	15:4	326
12:13	169	16:2	353
12:13	170	8:12	353
12:4-7	170	15:57	381
12:11	171	15:57	391
2:10-11	181		
1:2	185	## 2 Corinthians	
12:12-13	187	13:14	31
12:26-27	188	2:14a	44
6:19-20	190	5:17	46
12:28-31	197	5:21	52
10:31	198	4:5	74
2:9	202	5:21	138

Reference	Page
4:15	166
11:2	192
6:15	221
4:4	223
11:13-14	224
4:3-4	230
5:21	251
5:18-19	253
7:1	257
5:10	276
5:17	329
9:7	352
8:5	353
9:7	354
4:18	359
5:14-15	384
10:4-5	385

Galatians

Reference	Page
3:16	91
2:20	176
5:22-23	177
1:1-3	186
1:13	186
1:15-16	198
4:1-5	225
5:22-23a	365
2:20	382
5:16-17	387

Ephesians

Reference	Page
1:13-14	29
3:20-21	40
4:24	46
6:10-18	46
1:4	62
5:27	62
2:4	66
1:13	150,386
3:3-6	159
4:30	160
4:4-5	170
4:11	171
5:18	175
5:18b	177
4:30	178
5:18	179
5:25	186
3:3-6	187
2:8-9	189
2:19-20	189
5:25	190
4:11	197
4:12a	197
4:12b	198
4:11	205,206
2:8-9	213
2:2	223
6:12	226
6:16	228
6:11-12	233
1:7	245,252
1:3-4	256
1:13-14	265,275
3:21	271
1:13-14	275
1:20-21	301
2:8-9	330
3:20	371
5:26	373

6:17	375
1:13	386

Philippians

2:5-8	28
3:20-21	40
4:13	40
1:6	45
2:5-11	76, 97
2:11	166
3:20-21	273
2:6	324
2:7	324
2:8	325
2:9	325
2:10-11	325
4:19	358
3:7-8	385
3:3	388

Colossians

1:17	36
1:15-18	129
1:16-17	132
1:18	188
1:28-29	207
3:12	210
2:12	213
1:27	383

I Thessalonians

5:24	67
1:1	185
2:17-18	232
4:3,7	257
4:17	273
2:19	279
5:23	291

2 Thessalonians

3:3	67
2:3	288
2:3b	288
2:8	289

I Timothy

2:5-6	75
2:5	79
6:15	123
3:16	143
2:5	147
4:1	155
3:2	207
4:13	208
3:6	219
4:1	239, 242
2:1	344
6:9-10	355
6:17-18	357
5:8	358
4:13	369
1:1	383

2 Timothy

3:16	24
2:13	67
1:9-10	98
4:8	124
4:5	205
1:7	226

3:11-12	234
4:8	279
2:11-12	304
2:15	366
3:16-17	367
2:15	369

Titus

3:5	29,66
2:11-14	98
3:4-5	167

Hebrews

1:3	24
13:8	33
7:25	37
10:9-10	47
13:5b-6	51
4:15	51
13:5b	59
13:8	60
2:17	64,66
4:14-15	80
7:21-28	81
8:1	82
6:20	82
7:25	98
9:24	98
5:5	102
13:20-21	120
13:5b	137
13:8	137
7:23-25	137
4:15	138
4:14-15	142
4:15	145
9:14	181
13:7	209
13:17	209
9:11-12	252
7:25	263
2:5	303
12:22	318
7:25	338
13:15	340
7:25	344
13:16	357
5:13-14	366
4:12	367

James

1:17	33
5:4	48
4:7	228
2:19	238
2:10	247
1:12	279
4:13-15	356
1:21	364
4:6-8a	364
4:608a	364
1:23	372
1:18	372

I Peter

1:18-19	28
1:3	28
2:24	43
1:15-16	52
1:15-16	62

1:19-20	113
2:25	118
5:4	120
1:19	139
2:21	141
1:3	148
3:18	165
4:10	171
2:5	190
5:2	206
5:8-9	220
5:8	226
1:15-16	258
1:5	264
5:2-4	280
2:2	368
1:23	372
2:2	373

2 Peter

1:20-21	24
3:9	70
1:21	182
2:4-6	236
2:4	243
3:12	315
3:13	315
3:18	374
1:20-21	390

I John

3:20	57
1:1	60
5:11-12	60
3:5	62
2:1	63
2:2	65
1:9	67
4:15	76
3:8	89
4:15	90
5:10-12	90
5:13	90
5:20	90
2:2	99
4:9-10	102
2:2	114
3:5	138
3:8	141
1:9	161
1:7-9	178
2:14b	22
2:16-17	222
2:2	253
2:18	289
5:7	324
1:10	342
1:9	342
3:17	355
2:13	364
1:4	365

Jude

1:14-15	127
1:6	237, 243
1:24	261
1:14	296

Revelation

21:4	44

19:6	56	2:10	280
20:12	58	11:2-3	282
1:18	60	13:18	286
19:11	64	13:17	287
19:11	68	13:4	287
19:16	86	13:8	288
19:11-13	99	19:19	291
1:13-16	112	19:20	292
14:14	113	1:7	295
5:6-14	115	19:13	296
6:1	117	19:11	296
17:14	117	19:15	297
19:16	121	19:16	297
17:14	122, 123	20:2	297
19:16	123	11:15	302
22:12	126	20:1-3	304
20:11-15	126	20:7-8	305
19:11	128	19:16	306
19:15	128	20:7	310
1:8	128	20:8	311
1:17	129	20:9	311
21:6	129	20:10	311
1:18	132	20:11-12a	313
21:9	192	20:12	312
22:17	192	20:15	313
19:7-9	193	20:12a	314
22:18	199	21:10	315
1:3-4	201	21:3	316
12:9-10	220	21:2	316
12:9	223	21:10	317
12:10	224	21:16	317
2:9	231	1:3	371
12:10	232		
12:7-9	236		
16:13-14	240		

Breinigsville, PA USA
29 August 2009
223119BV00001B/2/P